PRIMARY

PROFESSIONAL BOOKSHELF

READING AND RESPONDING TO FICTION

classroom strategies for developing literacy

HUW THOMAS

Published by Scholastic Ltd
Villiers House
Clarendon Avenue
Leamington Spa
Warwickshire CV32 5PR

Author Huw Thomas
Editor Clare Gallaher
Series Designer Lynne Joesbury
Designer Clare Brewer

This book is dedicated to my father, with thanks.

Designed using Adobe Pagemaker
Processed by Scholastic Ltd, Leamington Spa

British Library Cataloguing-in-Publication Data
A catalogue record for this book is available from the British Library.

ISBN 0-590-53762-8

PRIMARY
PROFESSIONAL BOOKSHELF

CONTENTS

PRIMARY
PROFESSIONAL BOOKSHELF

ACKNOWLEDGEMENTS

I would like to thank the various staff groups who have encouraged me and enriched my experience as a teacher of literacy, in particular colleagues at Bushey First School and Poplar Primary School in London and those at Ellesmere First School, Byron Wood Primary and Springfield Primary in Sheffield. Also thanks to colleagues at Sheffield Hallam University. Particular thanks are extended to Gina Nuttall, Juliet Gladston and Clare Gallaher of Scholastic. I am also indebted to Anne Faundez, who suggested, 'You could do a book about this' and to Professor Nicholas Bielby who helped greatly during the writing of this work. Thanks also to David Clines and Anthony Thiselton for the early inspiration and to Kate and the kids, who have tolerated me during the writing process.

The publishers gratefully acknowledge permission to reproduce the following copyright material:

Material from the National Curriculum is © Crown copyright and is reproduced by permission of the Controller of Her Majesty's Stationery Office, 1995; extract from *The Cool Web: The Pattern of Children's Reading* by Meek, Warlow and Barton, Bodley Head; Quentin Blake illustration from *How Tom Beat Captain Najork and his Hired Sportsmen* by Russell Hoban and © 1974 illustration Quentin Blake, Jonathan Cape/Red Fox.

Every effort has been made to trace the copyright holders for the works reproduced in this book and the publishers apologise for any inadvertent omissions.

INTRODUCTION: SOMETHING TO DO WITH STORIES

This book is about stories. It's about doing things with stories. It's about the things we do when we read. It is also about things we can do to explore a story after we have read it.

It arose out of my own experience working with stories in the various classes I have taught throughout the primary age range. Stories are read in all primary classrooms but how can teachers take things further? The concept of doing things with stories can often frustrate teachers. There can be a sense of 'I've read it to them – what else can I do with it?' Frustrations like these can be prompted by external requirements, such as a programme of study or a school policy, requiring the coverage of certain aspects of stories. Such frustrations can also be prompted by the stories themselves, the sense that they contain so much that could be looked at in greater depth if only there were some guidance as to how to do it. This book is about how readers and texts interact; it's about doing things with stories.

NATIONAL REQUIREMENTS

The National Curriculum (DFE, 1995) outlines a specific set of requirements for work with story, placing before Key Stage 1 teachers the requirement that: *'Pupils should be given extensive experience of children's literature... from a range of genres'*; *'The materials read and discussed... should include... straightforward characterisation and plot'*.

It also requires pupils to *'talk about characters, events and language in books, beginning to use appropriate terminology'* and *'say what might happen next in a story'*. The English Language 5–14 National Guidelines (Scottish Office, 1991) also require pupils to *'Show that they know, understand and can use at least the following terms... character, setting the scene'*.

At Key Stage 2 the requirements state that texts used for reading should include those with *'more complex narrative structures and sustained ideas'* and that *'Pupils should be taught to consider in detail the quality and depth of what they read. They should be encouraged to respond imaginatively to the plot, characters, ideas, vocabulary and organisation of language in literature. They should be taught to use inference and deduction.'*

In addition, *'Pupils should be introduced to the organisational, structural and presentational features of different types of text, and to some of the appropriate terms to enable them to discuss the texts they read, eg author, setting, plot, format'*. Similarly, the Scottish 5–14 Guidelines require pupils to *'show that they know, understand and can use at least the following terms... plot, dialogue, main character...'*

The requirements mentioned above include an analysis of plots and characters, a look at some of the ways in which narratives are communicated, the use of a range of genres and a consideration of the response of the reader to the texts. These are all worthwhile objectives but they are demanding!

READERS

As well as the curriculum requirements, there is a requirement that comes from the children. The understanding of what they learn to read is a crucial part of their reading development. Over the past 15 years there has been a strong emphasis placed on the importance of meaningful reading of texts. The case for a move away from stilted scheme texts to 'real' books has been passionately made by educationalists such as Waterland (1985) and Meek (1988). This approach has effectively balanced the need for recordable progress in reading so that most schools now balance the use of schemes with a recognition that the love of story is also an essential part of learning to read. As well as the decoding of the print on the page, teachers encourage children to interact with the meaning of those words. This book aims to give some substance to phrases such as 'love of story' and 'interaction with meaning'.

CONVENTIONAL METHODS OF INTERACTING WITH STORIES

Reader-text interaction has a chequered history. The traditional comprehension exercise involved finding the right answers to a set of questions. These could often be completed without prompting interest or requiring understanding. Wray and Medwell in *Literacy and Language in the Primary Years* (1991) give an example of this, presenting the following passage:

> The chanks vos blunging frewly bedeng the brudegan. Some chanks vos unred but the other chanks vos unredder. They vos all polket and rather chiglop so they did not mekle the spuler. A few were unstametick. (page 141)

They pose questions about the passage, such as 'What were the chanks doing?', 'How well did they blunge?', 'Where were they blunging?' and 'Were any chanks stametick?' The fact is that many readers can answer a conventional comprehension exercise on a meaningless passage. This raises some doubts about the extent to which such exercises engage children with the meaning of texts. Instead of comprehending, the child may be just matching question to answer.

In the classroom there are a number of follow-up activities that are often bolted on to the reading of a story. The problem can sometimes be that these do not develop a meaningful interaction with the story. The classic example is the painting of a picture of a scene from a story. It may make for a good art activity, it may promote the story through a display and may serve as a concrete record of the child's memory of the story, but what it isn't necessarily doing is engaging the child any further with the story.

Similarly, the request to rewrite the story 'in your own words' seems a bit sterile, adding little, if anything, to the act of reading. It reminds me of the child who responded to the request by asking 'Why?' Simply re-presenting the story can prove frustrating for children.

There is also nothing more lethal to reading than 'death by a hundred book reviews'. One observation made in an OFSTED report (1996) into the teaching of reading was that:

> For some children the writing of a review for each book was demotivating and a hindrance to their reading because it was something which tempted them to finish the book slowly. (page 19)

There seems to be a gap in our provision for children working with the stories they know and the texts they have read. As teachers we are hot on the teaching of reading. The question is, what is to be done with the texts children are reading? Again, the OFSTED report into the state of the teaching of reading (1996) noted a curtailing of progress among children who had grasped the initial stages of learning to read. It was suggested that the problem may be one of motivation.

Clearly, there is a need to teach reading beyond the initial skills. This is not a new message. One of the troubling messages of the *Extending Beginning Reading* report by Southgate, Arnold and Johnson (1981) was the fact that competent readers did not know what to do with the skill once they had acquired it. The point was most graphically made by a child who was a confident reader 'but only wanted to master it "so that he could stop it"' (page 189).

The importance of engaging with the meaning of a text when it comes to the teaching of the initial skills of reading has been shown. What may now require some emphasis is the need to continue working on the meaning of a text rather than taking it for granted that it will automatically be interpreted.

LITERARY THEORY

Literary theory examines the content and make-up of literary works. It also looks at the interaction between the reader and the written text and the context within which this interaction takes place. A 'science of literature' called 'poetics' has developed. This has been defined by Hrushovski as 'the systematic study of literature as literature' (in *Narrative Fiction: Contemporary Poetics* by Rimmon-Kenan, 1983, page 2). It involves looking at the workings of texts such as stories and finding how the various elements in the text relate to each other. It involves looking at the ways stories are structured and the processes they undergo when they are narrated. It also involves looking at the role of the reader reading the story. One interesting definition of poetics is that provided by Adele Berlin (1983):

> If literature is likened to a cake, then poetics gives us the recipe and interpretation tells us how it tastes. (page 15)

As we read we interpret. We make sense of the text. We piece it together. We understand it. It has an effect on us. Interpretation is like tasting the cake. Berlin is suggesting that poetics, the study of the workings of literature, is like trying the cake and figuring out how it came to be the way it is.

This book suggests that there are some things inherent in stories that are worth analysing because they will send us back to the stories with a renewed perspective. An understanding of the workings of stories will stimulate the teacher's ability to develop an understanding and enjoyment of story in the children he or she teaches.

WHAT THIS BOOK DOES WITH STORIES

THEORY

This book develops the reader's awareness of some of the ways in which theorists have analysed literature over the past 30 years or so. However, it is not intended to cover the full breadth of literary theory. (The reader who wants to survey the subject more widely should look to books such as Selden's excellent *A Reader's Guide to Contemporary Literary Theory* (1985) or Rimmon-Kenan's *Narrative Fiction: Contemporary*

Poetics. Both these books have been of great use in the preparation of my own text.)

In addition, theorists mentioned in this book are not dealt with in full. The ideas of theorists change over time, and accounting for the twists and turns in their ideas would take up a whole bookshelf. I have presented the pieces of their work that have enlightened my classroom practice. I hope readers who find the ideas of a particular theorist interesting will refer to the bibliography for further material.

Finally, this book does not enter into the arguments between theorists. The differences between them are sometimes mentioned when relevant but, once again, space prohibits going into the arguments in greater depth.

To give a brief outline of how this book organises the areas of theory covered, Chapter 1 looks at the poetics of storylines and how a plot is structured, showing how events are linked together in a story; Chapter 2 looks at the characters involved in such stories; Chapter 3 focuses on settings; Chapter 4 outlines the process of narration, by which a story is communicated; Chapter 5 examines the concept of genre and looks at the range of stories used in the primary school; and Chapter 6 looks at the role of the reader in responding to stories.

WAYS OF READING

Theories explained in this book are not produced for theory's sake. They are there because they help us to understand the complexity of the reading process and, in doing so, help us to focus on some of the things that happen when readers read. Seeing what goes on when readers interpret a text can kit out an individual reader with different aspects of the reading process on which he or she can focus.

LEARNING OBJECTIVES

The essential task this book performs is that of showing how such theorising can contribute to children's learning. Focusing on different aspects of the reading process leads to the isolating of specific learning objectives that can feed into our literacy curriculum. Teachers reading this book may have an alternative set of objectives to which they are working, such as their school's scheme of work or the framework of a particular literacy initiative. Given that the material in this book deals with basic features of stories, there should be no conflict. The learning objectives in this book are meant to dovetail with those with which teachers are already working.

BOOKTALK

An understanding of how texts work can equip teachers with a more varied repertoire of ways of discussing stories with a class. By taking apart the different aspects of poetics on which such talk can be focused, this book should take the teacher beyond basic questions about a story such as 'What happened?' and 'Did you like it?'

ACTIVITIES

Each theoretical section of the book is supported by an 'In practice' section, which presents learning objectives and practical ideas to support the application of the theory in the classroom.

It is important that the activities are not seen as the end of the process. Many of them have arisen from reflecting on how work with specific stories can be stimulated by the theory outlined in the book. They are intended to start the reader off on the task of applying the theory to his or her own practice and the stories being used. The book should be a rod, not a fish.

CONCLUSION

The sort of approach to story promoted in this book can be used with any story. Unlike comprehension exercises that are linked to specific texts, the suggestions here will only really work if you take them and apply them to the texts of your choice. They should be the texts you know and for which you have some enthusiasm. It may be worth listing the ten books that feature most in your own classroom practice and seeing how some of the units of literary theory outlined in this book apply to those texts. How, for example, do they present characters? Do they feature varied points of view? To begin with it may be worth focusing on one of the earlier chapters on story or character, picking out the different aspects analysed and evaluating two or three favourite texts of varying length.

These aspects of what the book does and does not do all stem from the starting point of the classroom. In this book the classroom leads to the theory, not the other way round – but that's how it should be, isn't it?

CHAPTER 1

WORKING WITH STORY STRUCTURE

STRUCTURES IN STORIES

What do stories have in common? Not just two stories with similar setting or theme, but all stories – from *Jack and the Beanstalk* to *Star Wars*? The pursuit of some common underlying structures to stories has produced much of the theory that underpins this book. In the same way that there is structure in the grammar of sentences, theorists have tried to find a story grammar that structures stories.

If you look at a list of your ten favourite stories the commonality between them is sometimes obvious. A problem is set and then solved, a mystery is unravelled. Or, instead of seeking the truth, the characters seek a person or a treasure which they eventually find. They will present an issue that is worked through or a problem that is solved. There is a beginning, a middle and an end.

Vladimir Propp's *Morphology of the Folk Tale* (1968) was originally published in Russian in 1928. It provided a major contribution to the study of the commonality between stories. He analysed over a hundred folk tales and found a common set of functions underlying all of them. He defined a function as 'an act of a character'. He produced a list of basic actions that were common to the corpus of folk stories he analysed, showing how the stories drew on the same set of functions, always in the same order.

So in these stories a villain harms a member of a family; the act of villainy is followed by the hero being despatched on a quest; the hero is tested. Propp found the same functions repeated in the same order in tale after tale. Admittedly, he worked on a rarefied set of stories. There will be some difference between a Russian folk tale and a Quentin Tarantino film. Other structuralists, such as Bremond and Genette (who will feature in this chapter) and Greimas (who will feature in the chapter that follows), have developed schemas that aim to identify common structures within the workings of all narratives.

Drawing on the work of such theorists, this chapter will look at ways in which the teacher can gain a better understanding of the workings of a story, and use this understanding to promote the learning objectives presented throughout the chapter. This understanding can be built around the realisation that stories add events to events, combining such events and working through a series of possible outcomes. The chapter is divided into sections that look at:

- addition;
- plot;
- possibilities.

The section on addition examines the way in which event follows event in the story. This involves gauging the significance of various events and the part they play in the story, the way in which the events in a sequence can, in turn, be divided into smaller sequences of events and the way in which various stories arrange the order of events.

The section on plot explains the links between these events and outlines a way of understanding the concept of plot. This involves looking at the importance of the ending of a story.

The section on possibilities looks at the various alternatives presented in a story. This develops the understanding of the use of prediction and its importance in the comprehension of a story. It also leads to a look at the significance of the role of suspense.

From the outset, it must be stressed that the goal of such an enterprise is not the reduction of all narratives to a drab formula ('a task as exhausting... as it is ultimately undesirable', Barthes, 1977). As teachers of story, we should aim to use the insights such theory can offer to make the most of the texts we use in the classroom. By looking at the common structure in stories we can enhance our use of all the different stories we read in the classroom.

ADDITION

As a story unfolds progressively, one event is added to another. From the 'Once upon a time there was a boy called Jack' we expect a bit more. We expect things to alter in some way. The initial statement turns into a process, for example when the family starts to run out of food. Then the sale of the family cow by Jack for five beans is added on. As Cohan and Shires (1988) remark:

> The events constituting a story do not occur in isolation but belong to a *sequence*. Every sequence contains at least two events, one to establish a narrative situation or proposition, and one to alter (or at least merely to differ from) that initial situation. (page 54)

This process of addition can be seen vividly in the progress made by children in their story writing. As teachers, we look for addition. We look for the isolated line of news ('I went to the park') to become a sequence ('I went to the park and then I went to my friend's house and then we had an ice cream and then... and then...'). We look for children to move beyond writing the one-line event. We look for the sort of alteration that creates a story.

NUCLEI AND CATALYSERS

Event follows event as a story progresses, but each event differs in its significance. For example, a story could start with the sun shining and the birds singing on a lovely summer day. Then the Martians invade. Leave out the singing birds, forget the sun shining and the story is still on the move. Leave out the Martians and the story is nothing more than a sunny day waiting for something to happen.

In his influential essay 'Introduction to the Structural Analysis of Narratives' (1977), the theorist Roland Barthes makes a distinction between *nuclei* that 'constitute real hinge-points of the narrative (or of a fragment of the narrative)' and *catalysers* that 'merely "fill in" the narrative space separating the hinge functions' (page 93). These terms provide a helpful way of distinguishing between the significance of different story units. The nuclei are '...of direct consequence for the subsequent development of the story' (Barthes). They are the significant events that define the direction the story is taking. They maintain the course of events in a story, so that deleting one would involve altering the rest of the story.

Catalysers also perform important functions in a story. Although they are less consequential than the nuclei, the catalysers ought not to be seen as unimportant. They perform important functions. The difference is that they are of a lesser consequence in the development of the story. In Philip Ridley's story *Krindlekrax* (1991) there is a whole chapter in which the hero, Ruskin, is about to be told about the beast that lurks in the sewers under his street. This is a crucial disclosure, but each time the old caretaker, Corky, is about to tell Ruskin what cracks the paving stones and chars the brickwork, someone interrupts the conversation. The crucial disclosure is delayed. They meet the local landlord painting a pub sign, they buy some biscuits, they put the kettle on. If you removed any one of these interruptions from the story the crucial disclosure would still be revealed. The question 'What cracks the pavement?' would be answered. However, the pub-sign painting and biscuit buying are not unimportant. As the question remains painfully unanswered, these catalysers build up to the final line in the chapter. That is when Corky eventually answers the question. The interruptions butt into Corky's disclosure to Ruskin. They may also interrupt a teacher reading the chapter to a class. The resultant 'Oh, no!' when a class realises the disclosure is to be put on hold once again by another interruption vividly illustrates one of the functions such catalysers perform.

MICROSEQUENCES AND MACROSEQUENCES

Think of a favourite story. Try summarising it in five sentences. The chances are your summary will include the significant events in the narrative. 'Corky tells Ruskin a monster lives under their street' would be a more appropriate label for the section of *Krindlekrax* outlined earlier (page 16) than 'Corky buys a packet of biscuits'. The disclosure has more consequences than the biscuits. The process of addition involves the adding of event to event, but some events are more consequential than others. This notion of some events being more consequential than others implies some sort of hierarchy. The significant events we recount when we recall a story in summary form are made up of smaller sequences of events. Reading involves the recognition and naming of the events encountered in a story. The reader recognises a betrayal, a loss, a discovery. Any one of these events in a story can be made up of smaller events. Within your five-sentence summary, any one of those sentences probably covers a part of the story which is made up of smaller events.

In Diana Hendry's *Harvey Angell* (1991) the misery of Henry's life with his Aunt Agatha alters as a result of the new life that their lodger, Harvey Angell, brings into their home. We could label one section of the story 'Harvey arrives at the house'. That single sentence labels an event that takes up a whole chapter. We could label the next chapter 'Henry shows Harvey to his room', then 'Henry checks Harvey's references'.

Each of these event labels describes one of a series of events that could be related if we were describing the story in 15 sentences. Such a set of sentences would comprise a *macrosequence* that adequately related the gist of the story, providing a sequence of major events. However, in such a macrosequence each event label would describe a piece of the story that is made up of a series of smaller events. The label 'Harvey arrives at the house' is one part of a macrosequence. That part is itself made up of a set of events. The macrosequence can be broken down into a *microsequence*. So the label 'Harvey arrives at the house' is made up of a microsequence of events:

Harvey arrives at the house	Aunt Agatha introduces Harvey to Henry Harvey wanders around the kitchen, sniffing for 'connections' Aunt Agatha sends Henry off to peel the carrots Henry listens in on Aunt Agatha's conversation with Harvey

However, it must be remembered that each of these terms is relative. In the example above I could have taken events in the right-hand section as my macrosequence and broken down an event like 'Aunt Agatha introduces Harvey to Henry' into the microsequence:

Aunt Agatha introduces Harvey to Henry	Henry enters the kitchen Henry realises Aunt Agatha is sitting at the table with a stranger, *smiling* Aunt Agatha tells him the stranger is Mr Harvey Angell Harvey beams at Henry Henry beams back

How the hierarchy of macrosequence and microsequence is delineated depends on what you initially take as the macrosequence. For example, in Hugh Brogan's *The Penguin History of the United States of America* (1990) the Nixon presidency is one event in the macrosequence of the history. You could break that event down into its microsequence. In

Oliver Stone's film *Nixon*, the life of the President is the complete macrosequence within which Watergate features as an event that can be broken into a microsequence. In the film *All The President's Men*, the uncovering of the Watergate scandal is the macrosequence. The terms are relative. Inevitably the relative consideration of a sequence as a macro or microsequence will depend upon the parameters drawn around the sequence under consideration. One macro's micro is another micro's macro!

SEQUENCE AND TIME

The sequence of event added to event does not necessarily follow a strict chronological order. Many narratives make effective use of various ways of dissembling the time-scale that underpins a story. Quentin Tarantino's film *Pulp Fiction* opens with a scene in a bar. It then shows events that preceded the bar scene. It also shows events that will chronologically follow that scene before returning us to the scene in the bar at the close of the film. The strict chronology of events has been rearranged into a particular story sequence.

Gerard Genette (1980) has shown how the chronological order of events can be rearranged in a story. The order in which the events are related in the text can be in discordance with the order in which events occurred, a narrative device he labels *anachrony*. Genette demonstrates the existence of two types of anachrony. *Analepsis* occurs when the account of the story (the narrative) recounts an event that happened before the point we have reached in the story. We sometimes label such an example of anachrony a flashback.

A classic example of analepsis occurs in *The Frog Prince*. Once the frog has been transformed into a prince we hear that, many years ago, a wicked fairy turned him into a frog. He had to remain amphibious until a kiss released him from the spell. In other words, the story ends by relating an event that occurred before its beginning. Similarly, somewhere back in time, before the story of *Beauty and the Beast* the prince became the beast.

Before the story of *The Shrinking of Treehorn*, by Florence Parry Heide (1971), Treehorn stopped playing his board game, the 'Growing game', an event that caused all his problems. It is only after he has shrunk that he finds it and starts to play it again, thereby stemming his shrinking.

In Dyan Sheldon and Gary Blythe's *The Whales' Song* (1990) Lily sits with Grandma listening to her recount her childhood experiences of hearing the whales sing many years earlier. When, in Philip Ridley's *Krindlekrax*, the interruptions eventually stop and Corky the caretaker finally has the chance to tell Ruskin of his meeting with the monster that lives under their street, the story flashes back to a time before Ruskin was born.

The second, and less common, type of anachrony is *prolepsis*. Prolepsis involves an anticipation of events that happen after the time that is being recalled in the text. Genette points out the way in which first-person narratives lend themselves to this sort of anticipation. The narrator is recounting events after they have occurred, so will occasionally break with those events to anticipate what is to come. In Roald Dahl's autobiography *Boy: Tales of Childhood* (1984) he recounts visits he and his friend made to the sweet shop owned by Mrs Pratchett, whom Dahl describes as 'loathsome'. As the chapter ends, Dahl tells us:

> So you can well understand that we had it in for Mrs Pratchett in a big way, but we didn't quite know what to do about it. Many schemes were put forward but none of them was any good. None of them, that is, until suddenly, one memorable afternoon, we found the dead mouse.

As the next chapter opens we are taken back to a time before they hatched a scheme to frighten Mrs Pratchett with a dead mouse. Indeed, we are taken back to before they even found the mouse. What Dahl has done is hinted in anticipation. He's saying to his readers, 'Stick around – something gruesome is going to happen and it will involve a dead mouse.'

IN PRACTICE: ADDITION

In engaging with sequential ordering, the teacher is working on a concept that is fundamental to his or her work with children from nursery age onwards. Work on sequences introduces children to the language of abstract concepts such as 'first', 'last', 'before' and 'after'. It is a basic concept. It is also the reason why, in my class, Hamsa rushes to be first in the line or Amy loves to be last – there is something so important about the order and your place in it.

In looking at the sequencing of a story and examining the way in which addition works, we are reinforcing one of the principal pleasures of reading. Those who have worked with pre-school children will know how difficult it is to serialise a story. There is a burning desire to know what happens next and follow the story to the end. The adult who tries to break off the reading of the story faces the demand, 'You've started so you'll finish!' As children acquire understanding of the sequence that pulls along the reading of stories, our teaching should include learning objectives which foster this. Children should learn to:

✧ order a series of events in story form, either in their own writing or in work on stories;

✧ interpret the ways in which events in stories are added together in sequences;

✧ identify the main events that appear in a story sequence.

With such learning objectives in mind, there are various ways in which we can provide activities that focus on the sequences that make up stories.

WORKING WITH SEQUENCING

Learning about sequential ordering will reinforce a child's ability to order the events of a story. Many sequencing activities will reinforce this basic concept. It may be the ordering of numbers in mathematics or it may be the development of a gymnastic sequence in PE.

As far as stories are concerned, the most obvious sequencing activity is to reorder a set of sentences or pictures that make up a story. A number of photocopiable resources provide material for such an activity but a home-made version has the advantage of being able to be used for whichever story is the current favourite in the class. It works best with a set of four to six cards, each of which has a part of the story on it. This could take the form of a chunk of text you have copied out, but with younger children it can be more effective to present cards that sum up a section of the story. So instead of the following passage by Maurice Sendak in *Where the Wild Things Are* (1967) you could use a plain 'Max made mischief and was sent to bed'.

> The night Max wore his wolf suit and made mischief
> of one kind
> and another
> his mother called him 'WILD THING!'
> and Max said 'I'LL EAT YOU UP!'
> so he was sent to bed without eating anything.

It pays to vary the ways in which you present the story. Both ways serve different purposes. The summary gets to grips with the storyline but the copied-out section keeps the reader in touch with the language of the book.

To avoid sequencing cards being knocked out of place or dropped on the floor, it can be useful to fix them in some linear form. This gives a permanence, enabling them to be read and re-read as the sequence is considered and, if necessary, rearranged. By using Blu-Tack or pegging the sequence to a line, children can fix their ordering of events in a way that can be reviewed and altered.

THE 'NAIVE' TEACHER

When looking at children's attempts at sequencing it can be helpful to read the sequence aloud from the start and stop when muddled sections are encountered.

I recently read one group of children's sequencing of some story cards on the story *The Wooden Horse of Troy*. I read how the Greeks hid inside the horse. Then I read how they came out again. Assuming the role of naive reader, I asked 'What good will that do them?' We reasoned that they were still outside the city, climbing in and out of a big horse! At this point a child in the class realised that the card 'The Trojans wheeled the horse into their city' belonged before the part in which the Greeks leap out of the horse.

VARIED MATERIALS

Sequencing activities can involve a variety of materials. Practically any medium for the relation of stories can be used in creating a jumbled story that has to be sequenced to make sense. The following four examples demonstrate the possible variations that can be devised:

✧ Divide a story into six sections. Six children each read aloud a section of the story, but they read their sections out of order. Another group of children listen to the jumbled version, then move the readers around, ordering each section in a sequence until the reading of the story works smoothly. They should listen to the various attempts they make as they revise their ordering of the first group.

✧ A story is read in four short sections – each section being less than a paragraph – on an audio cassette. The sections are recorded out of order. Children then listen to the story and deduce how the mix-up can be readjusted (this will often involve making notes about each section).

✧ Comic stories, or cartoon sequences from strip cartoons, are cut up into separate sections. Sequencing these involves an interpretation of the underlying storyline, different combinations being attempted. The finished sequence is the one that makes most sense, and it is interesting to consider why other combinations do not work so well.

✧ Working at a computer using a word-processing or desktop publishing package, a story is typed out of order, then rearranged to make sense (this can be done using the 'cut' and 'paste' or 'mark' and 'move' facilities).

SEQUENCING AND ANACHRONY

Anachronic sequences can provide interesting raw material for a sequencing activity. In Chapman's *The Treasures of the Stone Lions* (1996), a book in the Heinemann 'Sunshine' scheme, Luke befriends some lion statues. Then, as he hides behind one of the lions, he overhears two robbers discussing treasure they have stolen and which they hid under one of the lions a year ago. This presents an interesting 'hitch' for children working on a sequencing activity as they try to decide where to place a card which has the description 'The robbers stole and hid the money'. Should they place it where it is discussed in the book or should it go before all the events (on the grounds that chronologically it was the first of the story's events to occur)? Would it be different if the card read 'The robber said he stole and hid the money'? Anachrony can be confusing! However, this is not a confusion to avoid. Coming into contact with such examples of analepsis not only demonstrates the narrative device, it also shows how so many of our stories are constructed on a foundation of events that preceded the time of the story.

EVENTS ADDED TO EVENTS

As well as sequencing events, children can analyse the different types of event that make up a story.

SPLITTING SEQUENCES

To explain to children that a section of a story's macrosequence can be split into a microsequence, it is best to start with an overview statement about what happened in a part of the story, either of your own devising or from a child. For example, when considering Sendak's *Where the Wild Things Are*, the response to the question 'What happened at the start of the story?' can prompt a reply such as 'Max went away to the land of the wild things.' Such statements can often be split. For example, 'First he was sent to his room', 'Then he went to the place of the wild things.' And then often split again. A chart that branches out can be a useful visual focus for this activity.

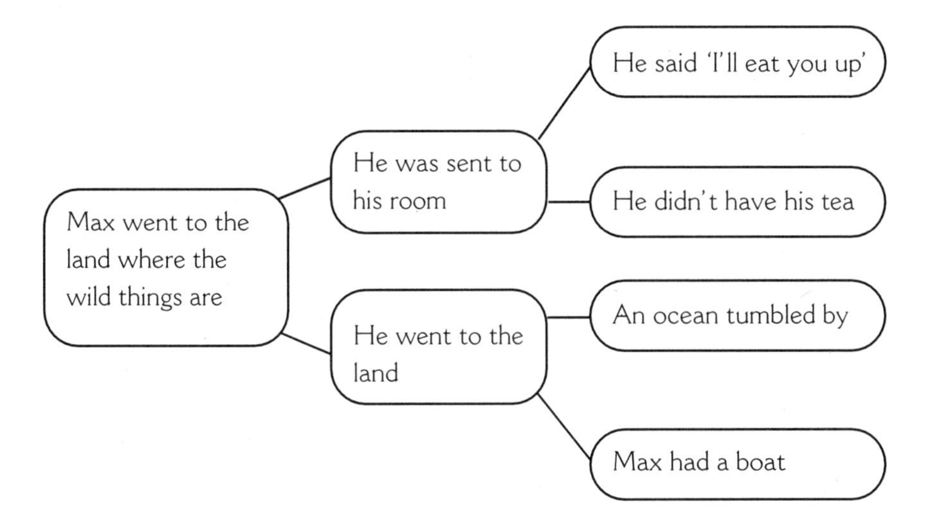

With younger children it is best to work through the process of splitting events, whereas older children can construct their own breakdown of events. In both cases, a picture book would provide the right sort of length of material.

BEFORE AND AFTER

On completing a story, the task of recalling the events is often tedious. Children sometimes don't know where to start or they all recall the same single event. One way of structuring the recollection of events is to label the middle of a large sheet with one sentence. This should recount one event from the middle of the story and acts as a marker.

Children then have to recall events that happened before and after that marker event (writing their suggested event on the sheet themselves or pointing to where it should be written). If it happened before the halfway event it should be written above the marker. If it occurred after, it should be written below. The example on page 26 shows how a group of children arranged events from Jan Mark's *The Snow Maze* (1992).

This idea can be refined so that events are distanced an appropriate space away from the marker event, as adopted in

Joah found a Key.
Irrum said i might open the lony Gate.
Joe found the maze.
Akmsh said "I dot Belive you."
pepole was ~~smiling~~ lughing at Joe
Irrum stood next to Joe.
Joe whanted to be brave like Irrum.
Irum saw Joe going thrght the Saet

Irrum sees the maze.

She runs the maze.
The Snow helped the children see the maze.
Akash sees the maze.
they but on sand
Akash was happy about the maze.
Joe put The Key in the long grass

the example shown above. While adding to this chart it is useful to re-read the list of events. Such a re-reading raises the question of the degree to which the summary of events that is being compiled matches the reader's overall memory of the whole story. Sometimes a crucial event will have been omitted. In the above example, one of the last events to be added was 'Joe found the maze', and yet it is the basis for all the events that follow it.

MAIN EVENTS

Given three pieces of paper to illustrate the three main events in *Cinderella*, which would children choose? This activity, using a longer story, scatters the focus from one single event. It is a variation on the old 'That's the story, now draw a picture of it' activity. By opening out the activity to a request for three events, interesting occurences from the breadth of the story can be recounted. (For example, I did this once with a first school class working on the nativity story. One child produced, as one of his pictures, a bearded man with a car. He told me 'That's Joseph and that's the taxi.' I was baffled for the rest of the day until I realised I had told the class 'Mary and Joseph went to Bethlehem because of the *taxes*.')

PLOT

In most stories the events are not just added together. Like a row of pearls, there is a thread that holds them together. Addition of event to event usually involves the combining of events into a sequence. The *combination* of the events is provided by the links between these events. Instead of pearls on a thread, they are like links in a chain. This combination integrates the series of events into a narrative that possesses an underlying *plot*.

Events can follow one another in simple succession and this succession of event following event can, in itself, be a strong link. For example, in Michael Rosen's *We're Going on a Bear Hunt* (1989) the characters progress through various types of terrain and weather, the link being that one obstacle in their bear hunt follows another as they press on through forests, mud, snowstorms and so on.

What many stories add to this succession of events is an underlying plot. A key feature of most stories is the way in which one event causes another. An understanding of the workings of cause and effect in stories can make a significant contribution to a child's development both as a reader and writer of stories. For the novelist E.M. Forster the *causality* at work in a story formed the defining element of the plot. Forster (1963) defined plot as 'a narrative of events, the emphasis falling on causality' (page 93).

The plot lies not in the succession of events but in the way one event causes another. Forster gives the example:

> 'The king died and then the queen died' is a story. 'The king died and then the queen died of grief' is a plot. (page 93)

A story can be a story without a plot. As readers we tend to expect some cause and effect between events in a story, but Cohan and Shires cite the example of *Alice in Wonderland* as a story in which event is added to event without the underlying causal links. The same could be said of Dylan Thomas's *Under*

Milk Wood (1954). In this 'play for voices', time passes through one spring day in a Welsh village, but the events that take place lack the link of one event causing another and the story lacks a plot.

In the first of Forster's examples, 'The king died and then the queen died', there is no stated cause and effect, just two events. The second example, 'The king died and then the queen died of grief', underpins this succession of events with a plot. It is the grief, the cause, that gives the story its plot. The events are combined by a cause (the king's death) leading to an effect (the queen's death).

In Forster's example, the link between the two events is clearly stated. Seymour Chatman (1978) points out that even if we were faced with the first story, 'The king died and then the queen died', we would think up a link between the two events; we would 'smell a rat' (two dead royals surely must mean a conspiracy?). We seek the link and assume that some cause and effect is at play in the succession of events. Rimmon-Kenan cites the example of:

> ...the witty account of Milton's life where the humour resides precisely in the cause and effect relation which can be read into the explicit temporal succession. Milton wrote *Paradise Lost*, then his wife died, and then he wrote *Paradise Regained*. (page 17)

In a way, such examples reinforce the importance to the reader of causality. It acts as a combining principle. We seek it even when it is not explicitly stated.

In a lot of children's literature the causality plays a major part in the unfolding of the story. Take, for example, the first line in Philip Ridley's *Kaspar and the Glitter* (1994): '"I'm getting worried now," Kaspar mumbled to himself.' It raises a cause and effect. What caused the worry? Whatever it was, what will happen? Are the worries justified? It is the sort of opening that hooks a young reader.

In Lewis's *The Lion, the Witch and the Wardrobe* (1950) the whole defeat of the evil witch by the children who enter the land of Narnia is triggered off by the English weather. It is raining. The children are indoors. This leads to a game of hide and seek. One of the children hides in a wardrobe and steps through it into Narnia.

The story needs such causal links. They are a part of the workings. In the same novel one of the children, Edmund, is persuaded by the white witch to betray his brother and sisters and abandon the side of good, led by the lion Aslan. As a result she owns him until he is released by the sacrificial act of Aslan. In one of the main events of the narrative the lion gives himself up to the white witch in exchange for Edmund.

This latter example illustrates the two ways in which Rimmon-Kenan sees causality at work in a story. If we ask 'Why did Edmund betray his brothers and sisters?' there are two possible answers. The straightforward one is 'Because the witch offered him a large amount of Turkish Delight if he joined her.' The other answer is that he betrayed his side because of what Rimmon-Kenan calls 'the structural needs of the plot' (page 18). Without that betrayal, Aslan and his side would have beaten the white witch in a fairly dull walkover. Add in the betrayal of Edmund and the plot thickens. How can Aslan win Edmund back? This example of what Rimmon-Kenan calls 'forward causality' creates a need in the plot that has to be fulfilled later on.

ENDINGS

'And they all lived happily ever after' – that's what so much of this is all about. The story is constructed in such a way as to work towards the ending. This concern with the eventual purpose (Culler uses the term '*teleological* determination') fuels so much of a story. Culler (1975) points out that certain things have to happen so that a story can develop towards the ending it possesses. Many events in a story are defined by this teleology. The part an event plays in the whole story defines that event. In a sense it is hard to know what an event is until you know how it contributes to the overall plot.

> After a severe quarrel hero and heroine may either be reconciled or go their separate ways, and the suspense which the reader might feel at such moments is, structurally, a desire to know whether the quarrel is to be classified as a testing of love or as an end to love. (page 211)

For example, in *The Whales' Song*, by Dyan Sheldon and Gary Blythe, Lily is prompted by her grandmother's reminiscences about hearing whales sing to spend all day on the jetty looking out to sea. No whales appear. Her uncle tells her to stop day-dreaming and orders her back into the house. We don't know if this is a disappointing confrontation with reality or an old man's irritability interrupting the young girl's confidence that her grandmother's magic will work. It is only as we read to the end that we understand which of these alternatives the exchange on the jetty really was.

In Terry Jones's *The Fly-by-Night*, one of his collection of fairy tales (1981), a little girl is visited by a strange creature travelling on a flying cat. The creature is a 'Fly by Night' who offers to take her flying. She accepts and the result is misery. Yet when Lucy, in *The Lion, the Witch and the Wardrobe*, enters the land of Narnia and accepts a faun's invitation to take her away to tea it is the start of a brilliant friendship. These are two similar events but one turns out to be an act of folly, the other a discovery of friendship. Both are eventually defined by the way in which the journeys develop.

The causality of the plot provides the 'because' that links events together. In Sendak's *Where the Wild Things Are*, Max was sent to bed because he 'made mischief'. He entered the forest because he was sent to bed. He found a boat because he entered the forest. He sailed to the land where the wild things are because he stepped into the boat. The plot needed Max to be sent to bed. The plot needed that forest to grow so that

Max could go from there, through the forest and reach the boat. According to the structural needs of the plot this was necessary in order that Max could enter the land of the wild things. Many such events are defined by outcome. An Agatha Christie story plays with alibis and red herrings in order that there may be a convoluted conclusion to the story. It is only in the last chapter that monogrammed handkerchiefs and misleading lies are finally set in the context that defines them, the ending.

IN PRACTICE: PLOT

So far we have seen how a story is made from events that add together to make a sequence. Causality combines the events into a plot. This combination is an important move. It is important for the story but it is also important for the understanding of a young reader. Seeing the links between events as one event causes another enhances the child's interpretation of the story. It enriches the pleasure and heightens the excitement as the story progresses towards an ending. For children developing their story writing, such a perception ties down the planning of stories. Children learn to link events and to make a coherent plot. As we work to explain plot, the learning objectives could be outlined as follows, namely that children should learn to:

✧ see the link between events in the stories they read;

✧ explain the causality at work in a plot, communicating their awareness of one event leading to another;

✧ link the events in their own stories into a combined narrative;

✧ unpick the ending of a story, pointing out the significance of events that caused the ending.

The following activities are examples of ways in which this causal link in the plots read in the classroom can be examined and explained. These practical ideas provide ways of looking at the combination at work in stories. As children look before an event to explain why it happened, or add extra sections in the form of plot boxes to develop an event to its next step in their own writing, they are working with the causal principle that can enrich their comprehension of stories.

ASKING 'WHY?'

The question 'Why?' teases out the link between cause and effect. It can furnish the reader with questions such as 'Why did the queen poison Snow White?', 'Why did Max go the place where the wild things are?' To move from asking 'What happened?' in a story to asking 'Why did it happen?' involves taking that step towards a grasp of the causality at work in a plot.

THE 'WHY' OF SEQUENCING

The link between events, one causing another, can fund the questions we put to children as they engage in sequencing activities. Returning to the Trojan Horse example used previously, I could have asked 'Why did they hide in the horse?' to show the problem with the disordered sequence. I find that when a group of children have done a sequencing activity the reasoning behind whatever sequence they devise is much more interesting than the sequence itself. It is not uncommon for a group of children to come up with an 'incorrect' result but also present perfectly good reasons for the incorrect sequence!

OPENING LINES

A collection of opening lines can present an interesting set of sentences, prompting questions such as the ones looked at earlier stemming from the opening of *Kaspar and the Glitter*. Other examples include:

> They say Maniac Magee was born in a dump. (from Spinelli's *Maniac Magee*, 1995)
> On the way to school Joe found a key. (from Mark's *The Snow Maze*)
> It was the day for choosing a hero. (from Ridley's *Krindlekrax*)

> Dear Greenpeace, I love whales very much and I think I saw one in my pond today. (from James's *Dear Greenpeace*, 1991)

Asking children what questions these lines provoke is sometimes so rewarding that the first reading time in the serialisation of a story is sometimes best begun with a reading of the opening lines, followed by the making of a list of questions they raise. These can be kept and looked at as the story progresses as we find out, for example, where Maniac was born, what the key does, why a hero is needed and whether there is a whale in the pond.

As teachers, we are limited in the amount of fiction we can read to children. When it comes to novels, a teacher may fit in one novel every half term. One way of broadening the amount of fiction we introduce into the classroom is to read selected opening chapters. Often a child who hears the opening chapter of a story will want to read the rest. Reading an opening chapter of a story once a week or reading the opening pages (or even just the opening lines) of a few picture books during a library session are activities that can 'hook' the young reader.

WORKING BACKWARDS

Start with an ending. It could be one from an actual story or a line made up for the activity. For example:

> The girl found the lost shoe.
> The monster ran away.
> The spell wore off.

The task is for children to work backwards from that ending to produce a set of events that could have led up to the ending. The more complex the ending the harder it will be to tease out the process that satisfies the structural need for events that cause it. Take the following lines as an example of a made-up ending of a story.

Then the prince woke up,
Saw the spider
And screamed,
But it was too late,
There was nobody left to hear him!

What could have led up to that?

LINKS

This can be tried with a part or the whole of a story. The idea involves drawing a series of linked circles and working from one event through the causal relationship that connects it with other events. The links can vary in number as can the nature of the event provided. It could be a note from the start of a story with the requirement that a reader or a group of readers find the effect of that cause, as in the example below, which gives the first link drawn from Shirley Hughes's *Dogger* (1977).

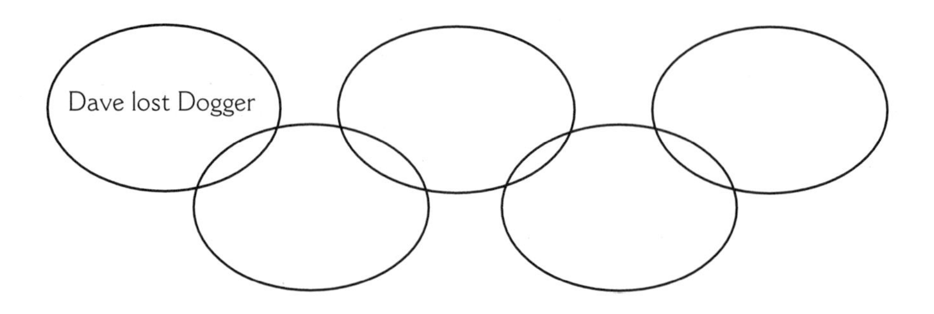

Or an effect for which the causes must be provided.

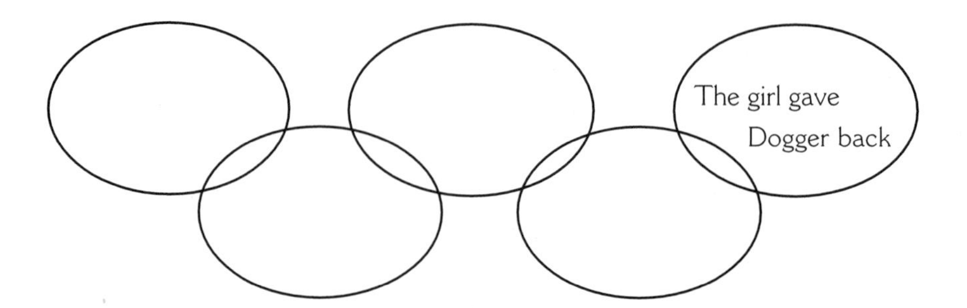

In the previous example the children have to work back from the ending of the story.

Another strategy is to use an event that is central to the combination. This would require working out the causes and the consequences of that event.

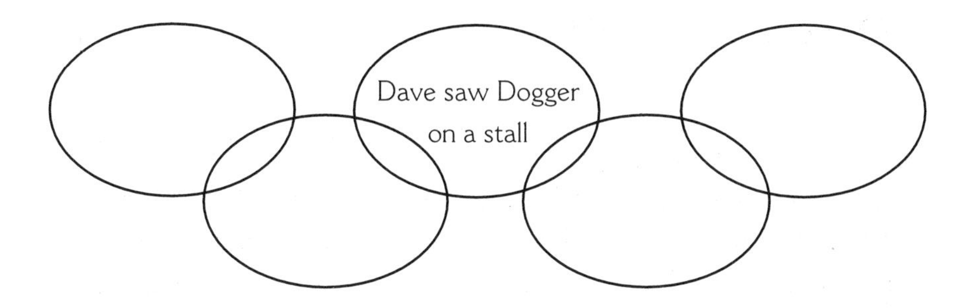

There is something graphic about these links that reinforces the link between one event and the others with which it is combined.

PLOT BOXES

With some children, I have often found the process of story writing to be an uphill struggle. There is the story that rattles along and goes nowhere:

> Then the girl went to the shop and then she went to the park and then she saw a girl and the girl went to the shop and then went to the park and they both went to the shop and went to the park...

There is the awful anticlimax:

> I went to visit my friend. He opened the door. He asked me in. His house seemed strange. I went into his kitchen. The air suddenly felt cold. I looked round but he had vanished. There was a creaking noise on the cellar stairs. Suddenly I heard a scream.
>
> Then I went home and had my tea. The end.

I originally started using plot boxes to develop some of the descriptions and extend some of the endings in stories written by children I taught. However, they have also proved to be a useful way of developing an awareness of the links children can produce in the stories they plot.

Each child is given five pieces of A5-sized paper and asked to write a story spread over these five sections, working towards pasting the boxes on to a larger sheet of paper. They are urged to change to a new piece of paper, making another box, if one significant event is leading to another. If the theft of a shoe is about to cause someone to miss a bus, or the mixing of a magic powder with water is about to cause a monster to appear, they change to a new box. The story is written, box added to box, and the set is kept in an envelope. (Some children may find that they need more than five boxes.) Between the completion of the boxes and the pasting of them on to the larger sheet, there is a conference. The teacher reads through the story and looks for the points where an extra box could be inserted.

Returning to the examples given on page 35, an extra box could explain how the two girls in the park started talking and ended up going to the shop together or it could extend the second example so we find out what why there was a scream. Once the additional boxes have been inserted, the story can be pasted on to the larger sheet of paper.

These plot boxes provide a way of working with the events in a story, editing and refining them. They release a child who has completed a story to work on the story's key events.

POSSIBILITIES

Between the beginning and end of a story there is a plot that combines the events in a sequence. The course of one event leading to another unfolds as the story progresses. However, if the course of events were predictable and obvious from the outset the events would lose the power they have to disclose what happens. So nothing is certain. If William Tell misses the apple the child is killed. This uncertainty, the way the events unfold and are discovered as we read, is a major part of the pleasure of stories and something we can make the fullest use of as we engage children in the task of examining the workings of a story.

THE NETWORK OF POSSIBILITIES

In a story the events are forged out of the wealth of possibilities. Mark Lawson's novel *Idlewild* (1995) is an account of the lives of John F. Kennedy and Marilyn Monroe in an imagined modern-day setting they both survived to see. He tells how the priest preparing to administer Kennedy's last rites following the unsuccessful assassination attempt in Dallas in 1963 experiences:

> ...a sudden sense of this moment as one of history's hinges. Events can swing to either side from here. (page 10)

Kennedy lives. The priest is sent away. Lawson's story is triggered by events taking a unique turn that comes as a surprise to the reader.

The events that come between the opening and ending of a story form a pathway through a series of possibilities. These alternatives disrupt the equilibrium at the start of the story. When Alfie comes home in Shirley Hughes's *Alfie Gets in First* (1981) he could have just walked straight into the house and all would be well. But because he slams the door he is locked inside with Mum on the outside. This provides a problem and becomes a story.

Throughout a story alternatives present themselves and the story follows one of the possible paths. Jack could sell the cow to the man offering five beans or he could take it to the market. The beans may grow or they could waste away outside Jack's window. Jack could climb the beanstalk or he could stay safely at the bottom.

In his article on 'The Logic of Narrative Possibilities' (1980) Claude Bremond analyses the elementary sequences at work in narratives and shows how the possibilities follow a pattern:

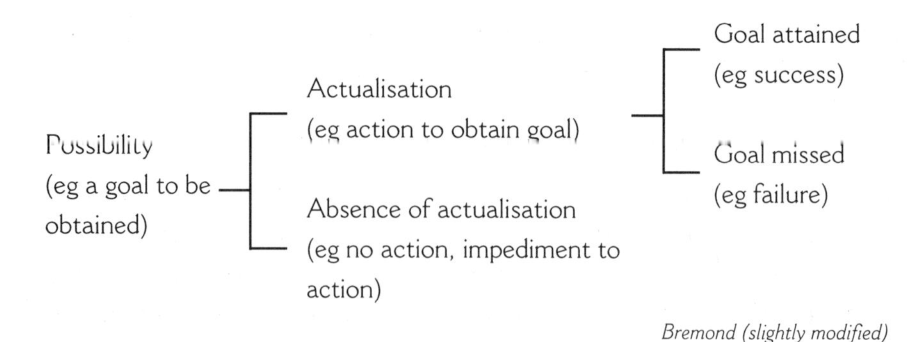

Bremond (slightly modified)

Bremond uses the phrase 'the network of possibilities' to describe the way in which the narrative is made up of basic units in which there is a sense of the 'possible'. Events presage other events (or to quote the subtitle of Lawson's alternative history *Idlewild*, 'Everything is Subject to Change'). Earlier we looked at the teleological determination at work in a story. This is a deciding factor in the direction the story takes. When the magic beans sprout Jack is presented with a possibility: climb up the beanstalk. Jack could choose not to climb the beanstalk but if he doesn't actualise the possibility presented by the beanstalk then he and his mother will have a big plant on the front lawn and starve to death! The absence of actualisation would not make for much of a story.

We saw earlier the distinction Barthes makes between nuclei and catalysers in the sequence of a story. The definition Barthes gave of the nuclei was that they 'constitute real hinge-points'. The nuclei open up the network of possibilities in the story. What is often interesting is the number of possibilities opened up in these nuclei. They can form a focus for discussion along the lines of 'What should Jack do about the Beanstalk?' He could climb it, cut it down, cultivate the beans. If he were Aunt Sponge and Aunt Spiker from Roald Dahl's *James and the Giant Peach* (1967) he would charge admission to view it. The network of possibilities is open.

The array of possibilities is the raw material we draw on in making our predictions as to what will happen in the story. As we read on, we work on these predictions, narrowing down the array of possible outcomes into the probable outcomes and, eventually, the actual outcome.

PREDICTION AND COMPREHENSION

Prediction is an important part of the enjoyment of a story. The cliffhanger endings of soap operas work by leaving the viewer with a range of possible outcomes. The viewer knows the wife has picked up the bread knife when she sees her husband kissing the woman in the car, but the signature tune interrupts and you are left knowing the knife will be used – but not on whom. The husband? The woman? The bread? What the viewer knows creates an array of possibilities.

Prediction also plays a large part in a reader's enjoyment of a story. In *Rosie's Walk* (1968), by Pat Hutchins, Rosie the hen sets out on her walk. We see the fox following her. We can predict two things that could happen. The fox could get her or the fox could fail. From these predicted possibilities the reading of the story gains a momentum. Faced with a plain picture of a hen going for a walk the reader could so easily give up reading with the comment 'So what?' but in this story the reader's attention is held by the possibilities.

As well as being important for the momentum, prediction also plays an important part in our understanding of a story. Frank Smith (1985) defines comprehension as a state of fulfilled prediction:

> Prediction is asking questions – and comprehension is getting these questions answered. (page 83)

Going back to Rosie the hen, as soon as she sets out on her walk the reader will predict that there will be an outcome. The fox won't simply follow the hen. Experience of other stories trains readers in their expectations. A sentence such as 'I caught the train to' is incomplete. We know it is because we understand how such sentences work. We are schooled in predicting that there should be a bit more. That bit more could

be the train's destination. It could also be a word like 'escape' or 'relax'. It is unlikely to be 'went' or 'spoon'. We know enough about the structure of sentences to predict the sort of thing we expect to come next.

Prediction sets up the expectation that develops understanding. Knowing where the story is going enables the reader to comprehend it as it is being read. Therefore, as we work with children's reading of stories, prediction is a significant skill to foster. As a child reads, prediction lays the groundwork for comprehension of what comes next. The reader knows what sort of results could be expected from the fox's pursuit of Rosie. That lays the groundwork for following the various ways in which the fox is frustrated and finally thwarted. In working with children's predictions, asking them what will happen next and working on the reasons that lead to their prediction, we are building up a skill that isn't just a way of anticipating the next page of a story or placing a bet. Prediction plays a vital role in the understanding of a story. Chatman presents us with an insight that is not unlike Smith's idea of the 'elimination of unlikely alternatives':

> ...the working out of plot (or at least some plots) is a process of declining or narrowing possibility. The choices become more and more limited, and the final choice seems not a choice at all, but an inevitability. (page 46)

DISPLACEMENT

Between the possibility that opens a story and the outcome that concludes it there is a space filled by other events. To take the story of *Jack and the Beanstalk* again, Jack's family is starving. Suppose his Uncle Ernie dropped off a load of food and solved the problem – the story would be an anticlimax. Such an outcome is too straightforward. What many stories present is the postponement of the outcome. The addition of other events that complicate the initial situation generates an interesting displacement of the initial situation. If Jack makes a rash decision to sell the cow for five beans, a beanstalk appears and Jack climbs it, the macrosequence between the opening problem and the final outcome of the story is widened. Cohan and Shires explain this *displacement* in the following way:

> ...when a story sequence combines more than two events (and most do), the addition of other events advances or amplifies the sequence to widen the space between opening (i.e. the possibility of an outcome) and ending (i.e. the realization of an outcome). (page 65)

> ...what initiates a story is the *placement* of an event in a sequence to mark a beginning; what ends a story is the *replacement* of the initial event by another one to mark an ending... what keeps the story going as a sequence of eventualities are *displacements* of both the initial and the closing events. (pages 65–66)

The beginning and end of the story are separated by the displacement that lies between these two events.

SUSPENSE AND SURPRISE

The gap between expectation and fulfilment provides the potential for the reader to be kept in suspense. School residentials wouldn't be the same without the late-night story, the story that builds up chilling events. The 'campfire' tale revels in the lapse between expectation and fulfilment. 'The man steals the ring from the skeleton. Later that night he hears the footsteps on the stairs. Paff! Paff! Paff! The door creaks open... Creeeeaaakkk! A wiry figure edges closer to the bed and holds out a bony hand. The fingers unfold... Crick Crack Crick Crack...' Children are wide-eyed and petrified, willing you to tell them what happens to the man. Their expectation is not immediately fulfilled. The delay they are experiencing is called *suspense*.

This is different from surprise, when an unexpected event leaps out of a story, catching the reader unawares. Suspense works on expectations. One of the finest definitions of suspense is that given by the film director Alfred Hitchcock in Truffaut's *Hitchcock* (1978). Asked by a questioner to define the difference between suspense and surprise he responded:

> ...suppose that there is a bomb underneath this table between us... There is an explosion. The public is *surprised*... Now, let us take a *suspense* situation. The bomb is underneath the table and the public *knows* it... The public *is aware* that the bomb is going to explode at one o' clock and there is a clock in the décor. The public can see that it is a quarter to one... The audience is longing to warn the characters on the screen... In the first case we have given the public fifteen seconds of *surprise* at the moment of the explosion. In the second case we have provided them with fifteen minutes of *suspense*. (page 80)

An awareness of this effective device will inform our reading and telling of stories. When Hitchcock speaks of the public being informed of the situation beforehand, the principle is important as we introduce children to the use of suspense in the stories read in class. It involves making sure the reader or listener is informed and expectant, then prolonging the agony.

Similarly, when reading or telling stories the effective use of surprise is valuable. I remember on a recent residential weekend telling a late-night story in the fire-lit sitting room. In the story the man, alone in the house, believed that the monster who knocked on the windows before it got you had gone away for good. My voice was at a whisper as I said, 'But just then...' At this point, Esther, my collaborator, who was planted outside and listening for her cue, rapped like thunder on the window. The effect was worth all the planning and an awareness of the subtle difference between suspense and surprise paid off. Who said literary theory was dull?

IN PRACTICE: POSSIBILITIES

If Cinderella had had a balanced and happy home, then automatically married the prince, there would be no misery, no godmother, no midnight clock and no glass slipper. We would be left with a bland tale of upper-class marriage. The possibilities that open up in a story make all the difference, and we are drawn to them.

These possibilities make up an important part of a child's reading development. In introducing young readers to the array of possibilities that are opened up within a story, we are working at the nub of a child's interest and enthusiasm for stories. More specifically, we are getting down to the following learning objectives. Our aim is that children learn to:

✧ understand the array of possibilities opened by a story and the way in which these possibilities narrow down into probabilities;

✧ make and support predictions when reading a story;

✧ reflect on the points at which alternative possibilities were available and a particular alternative was selected.

The activities outlined below pick up this theme of possibilities, looking at how children can move from an awareness of the possibilities present in a story to a prediction as to what course of action is probable followed by comprehension of what actually happened.

ALTERATIONS

Children can be asked to look at the scenario in a picture (select one that has some potential for being turned into a storyline) and offer suggestions as to how it could alter. What could happen next? Advertisements in magazines can provide good raw material. A man is meeting a woman and handing her some flowers. What could happen next? Is she pleased with the flowers? What if she isn't? Who else could walk in on this scene? What will happen when the third party appears?

In taking a particular situation and altering it, the children are displacing the original placement. All possibilities should be allowed (for example, 'She is an alien', 'She will eat the flowers'). The wackier they are the more they teach the point that a story opens up a network of possibilities.

A variation on this activity is to think of a routine event and disrupt it. For example, the bell goes at quarter past three, we are collected and we go home. What if one day the bell didn't go? What if we were not collected? Or take another norm such as gravity. What if gravity were disrupted?

LOOK FOR DISRUPTION

An obvious way of focusing on the possibilities that open up in a story is to look at the possibilities that are presented in some of the stories we encounter. One way of doing this is to ask a small group or a class to look at the same story. After reading the story they are to look for the initial situation. It may be a simple case of a child walking round the house being ignored, as in David McKee's *Not Now, Bernard* (1980). The critical point you are asking the children to find is the one at which they believe the disruption that makes for a story started. At what point do things start to change (for example, Bernard says there is a monster in the garden)? They could mark this point in pencil or place a bookmark at the page. Once they have formed their personal opinions ask them to compare notes. They will possibly differ. On looking at Dahl's *James and the Giant Peach* some will define the initial situation as being James's idyllic home life with his parents disrupted by their death. Others will mark life with Aunt Sponge and Aunt Spiker as the opening norm and define the escape into the peach as the point of disruption.

Within these varied results the concept of the displacement that disrupts a situation and makes for a story is being reinforced.

POINTS OF CHANGE

Following the reading of a story, the children can be asked to find three or four points at which the story changed. The task requires an examination of the points at which the story took a particular direction.

These nuclei will provide the sort of hinge-point that Barthes (1977) discusses. Children can often generate an array of imaginative possibilities as to what could have happened in any situation. I sometimes find they are freer to do this once they have finished reading a story. When they know how the action progresses they are often less inclined to cling to their chosen prediction and more ready to entertain the idea that a lot of other possibilities could have stemmed from one of the nuclei in a story.

WHAT IF...?

A life story, yours included, is riddled with 'What if...?' occurrences. What if you hadn't been in that particular place at that particular time? What if your parents had never met? What if you had not become a teacher? (Don't dwell on that last one.) These can be fascinating questions and can provide pointed insight into the development of a story. Finding a point in the story and asking 'What if...?' leads to a comparison of the possibilities that were on offer in a story with the eventuality that actually took place. A question like 'What if Max (in Sendak's *Where the Wild Things Are*) had not been sent to his room?' highlights the way in which the possibility that was followed gave us the particular story we read. For younger children this question provides an easy way of taking apart the events in a story.

The 'What if...?' questions can be given to the children or they can be encouraged to make a list of their own. The latter usually involves them in a consideration of the results their questions illuminate.

This activity has interesting links with analepsis. If we take a story such as Parry Heide's *The Shrinking of Treehorn* as an example, at the end of the story we discover Treehorn started to shrink because he stopped playing and lost his 'Growing game'. This event preceded the story and is related out of its chronological sequence. A question such as 'What if Treehorn had carried on playing the "Growing game"?' demands a reordering of the events in the story as well as a consideration of the effects that the events caused.

This activity provides a healthy alternative to the tired activity, 'Write the story but change the ending'. Such a request can provoke the response 'Why go to the bother of writing a whole new ending? The one we had is there for a reason.' Alternatively, by getting to work on the 'What if...?' possibilities in a story, children analyse the ending provided. They consider how the story works towards the ending it has.

DISPLACEMENT

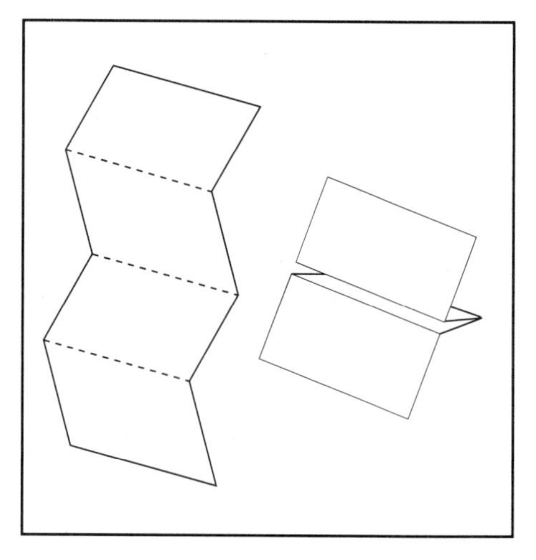

If the children are asked to select a story, they can then write or draw the beginning and the end of the story: a piece of A4-sized paper is folded horizontally into four sections, as shown.

This creates a physical gap between the first section (the beginning) and the fourth section (the end). The children are asked to focus on the situation placed before them at the opening of a story and the situation that replaces it at the end. Then the paper can be opened out and the two sections compared. In the middle section the children can jot down some of the differences between the situation placed in the top box and the situation that replaces it in the bottom box. A displacement has occurred in between. This activity gives a visual form to that transformation to enable the child to see it at work.

PREDICTION

We saw earlier the importance of predictions in reading and comprehending a story. It can be worthwhile recording predictions and keeping them. They can be matched to the outcomes in the story to see how close to the actual text they are. I recently read the opening of Jan Mark's *The Snow Maze* to a class. In the opening, when Joe finds an old key, there is a hint that the key will be special and Joe is most protective of it. I asked the children to predict what the key would do. The predictions were:

> Open a magic box.
> Take him flying somewhere.
> Open a magic door.
> Make a spell for the boy.
> Take him into a magic maze.

As the class carried on reading the story they found that the key opens a magic gate that leads to a lost maze. But the list was worth retaining because when we got into the story we found, firstly, that there was definitely an element of magic to the key, something that featured in all the predictions. Secondly, we found how close the last prediction was. A combination of the idea that a key opens something ('Take him into') with the sense that the story is magical ('a magic') was added to a word from the story's title ('maze') to give us a fairly accurate prediction. Having listed such predictions, we read through the story, comparing them with the outcome.

PROBABILITY

The scale of probability used in maths can also be used in looking at stories. The current national curricula for maths at Key Stage 2 include the requirement to teach the way in which the probability of any event lies between the 'impossible' and the 'certain'. Along this continuum there are many categories, spreading outwards from 'even chance':

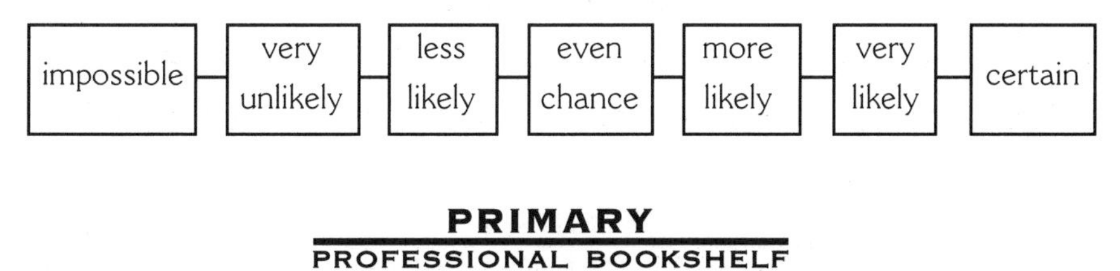

Probabilities can be gauged by placing possibilities along this continuum. As a story is read and predictions are made, children can use this scale as a means of gauging the likelihood of their prediction being fulfilled. As we meet Kathryn Cave's friendless character Something Else in the opening pages of the book of the same name (1994), children may feasibly predict that he will form a friendship with the other creatures who originally shun him. He may save them from danger or appeal to their better nature. However, when it comes to placing it along a line of probability, the likelihood of the prediction occurring has to be considered. It isn't certain. It isn't impossible. It could be seen as an even chance (though in actual fact he never does build up such a friendship). The probability scale ties down the prediction. It rules out the impossible and recognises the certain. We could rightly predict that Something Else will find some happiness and rate that prediction as very likely. We could rule out Something Else being eaten by vampires as very unlikely. The scale provides a step beyond prediction.

I have used a line of string and asked groups of children to come up with predictions. I have then worked with a larger group pegging the predictions along the line of probability. The activity takes the varied predictions children can offer and uses what is known from a story as a means of rating the likelihood of certain predictions. (Of course, you could develop your probability scale to the stage where you give odds on the outcome of the story!)

MAKE THE MOST OF SUSPENSE

Reading a story beforehand can help with the task of finding the points where suspense can be used to its fullest effect. These may be the points at which you close the book and say, 'We'll finish that story off tomorrow' or the ones that you build up gradually, eking out the tension. Exploit the story's atmosphere because this teaches more than a device called 'suspense'; such an experience of the thrill of stories gives childen the motivation that makes them want to read.

CONCLUSION

Stories share a number of characteristics. An understanding of the workings of some of these structures can enhance the teacher's work with the stories that are read or told in the classroom. In a story the process of addition is developed by the plot that links events together. A pathway is forged through a network of possibilities. It keeps the reader in suspense, wanting to find out how the initial situation is replaced. The guesses we make as we read are confirmed or dashed as we forge ahead.

CHAPTER 2

CHARACTER

Think of a character. Any character from a story you read, heard or saw more than a year ago. Now imagine this character coming up to you, wherever you are reading this book. Look at the character. The character looks at you. What, if anything would you say? What about the character? What would he or she (or it) do? What about your feelings? They will vary. Those of you meeting Peter Pan will have different responses to those currently in the same room as Hannibal Lecter! Different readers will respond to different characters in different ways.

What does the fact that you could imagine a character there with some sort of independent existence tell you about this element of a story that we call 'character'? Characters are fictitious, they are 'made up', yet we can imagine them as persons.

In the Introduction to this book various requirements from the national curricula were noted. These include requirements to teach about characters and characterisation. This is also a requirement that runs through the guidelines of the National Literacy Project (1997). The project guidelines highlight work on character as one of the 'recurring themes in the text level objectives' (page 10).

In teaching children about character we are providing them with an exciting insight into the workings of stories. This chapter demonstrates how an understanding of the way in which texts work can enrich the understanding of character. After examining what is meant by character, outlining two debates which open up the idea of 'character' and showing ways in which we understand and appreciate it in our reading of the story, we will look at four character-related terms – traits, paradigm of traits, characterisation and role – around each of which some insights into character can be clustered. As with Chapter 1, there will be an excursion into theory followed by the provision of some learning objectives that stem from the theory, and practical ideas for taking these ideas further into the classroom.

THE CONCEPT OF CHARACTER

Like many terms in literary theory, character is one that appears to be quite straightforward. Expressions such as 'He's a shady character' or 'the film's use of cartoon characters' develop the use of the term in everyday speech. However, this simple term contains some complex ideas.

The following two debates examine some of the issues raised at the very outset of a discussion of character. They show the complexity of the concept we are looking at. They also introduce a way of looking at character that needs to underpin our work in the classroom.

THE 'BEING OR DOING' DEBATE

For many of us, as readers, characters are an integral part of a narrative. In the previous chapter we looked at the action that takes place in a narrative. Characters are involved in doing much of that action.

Some literary theorists have taken an extreme view of the 'doing' functions of characters in stories, to the point of saying that the characters are secondary to the actions they perform. Barthes (1977) notes that:

> From its very outset, structural analysis has shown the utmost reluctance to treat the character as an essence, even merely for purposes of classification. (page 105)

Characters are seen as functional. Their only importance lies in the actions they perform to move the important element, the plot, along. There has been a tendency in structuralism to react against any idea of characters as being somebody and having a personality. Jonathan Culler gives the following explanation in *Structuralist Poetics* (1975).

> Character is the major aspect of the novel to which structuralism has paid least attention and has been least successful in treating. Although for many readers character serves as the major totalizing force in fiction – everything in the novel exists in order to illustrate character and its development – a structuralist approach has tended to explain this as an ideological prejudice rather than to study it as a fact of reading. (page 230)

In other words, there has been a tendency for certain thinkers to ignore who characters *are*, this being dismissed as a bourgeois romanticising of their individual role. Instead, the emphasis has been squarely placed on what they *do*.

This will sit uneasily with many readers because we don't come away from reading stories feeling that characters are just things that do things. There will always be characters who feel like real people, and readers will consider their encounter with characters to be more than just an inventory of what they did to further a particular storyline. There is something important about their being, about who they are: '...though fused with the action... they are not dissolved in it' (page 122 in Martin's *Recent Theories of Narrative*, 1986). They retain something identifiable and distinct.

However, while wanting to hold back from the extreme position of relegating characters to mere functional levels, we can gather an important message from this extreme position. As we look at characters we need to look at their significance in the workings of the plot. This will be particularly important for the section of this chapter that asks 'What do they do?' As we look at structuralist diagrams of character functions and actions in a plot we will see how important the things they do are in defining their role within the story as a whole.

THE 'OPEN OR CLOSED CONSTRUCTS' DEBATE

The second debate raises the issue of what it is appropriate to ask about characters. If you think of them as beings, to what extent can you speculate beyond what you are actually told about them in the text? Are they closed or open constructs? Let me define the two possibilities.

CLOSED CONSTRUCTS

This option leaves us with characters operating in a text, doing what they do in a story – and that is that. You can't ask questions about them beyond what you find out within the closed world of that story. For example, James Henry Trotter's life with his parents is restricted to the first page of *James and the Giant Peach*. Characters are what they are in the text. There is no room for speculation about James's life before the story started. He starts when the story starts. This option closes off the possibility of any further speculation. As J.M. Cameron remarks:

> We cannot ask how many children Lady Macbeth had; or what courses Hamlet pursued at the University of Wittenberg. (in Chatman, page 117)

OPEN CONSTRUCTS

This option leaves characters open to further speculation. Obviously this will have certain limitations. No one will come up with a definitive résumé of James Henry Trotter's life before his parents were eaten by the rhinoceros (Dahl, 1967). However, images conjured up by the assurance in the story that his life was peaceful and that he lived beside the seaside give speculative licence to creative readers. Such speculation led to an extra scene for the film version of this story in which James is seen playing on the beach with two ideal parents, sharing dreams of their future.

Chatman criticises the closed viewpoint, asking:

> In short, should we restrain what seems a God-given right to infer and to even speculate about characters if we like?

> Any such restraint strikes me as an impoverishment of aesthetic experience. (page 117)

He goes on to recommend what he sees as the correct option:

> A viable theory of character should preserve openness and treat characters as autonomous beings, not as mere plot functions. It should argue that character is reconstructed by the audience from evidence announced or implicit in an original construction... (page 119)

In teaching, this open view is, to my mind, essential to the development of creative, responding readers who experience in their reading a series of encounters with characters with whom they engage. The balance offered by this mini debate is the need to see such engagement as dependent on the evidence in the original construction. The character we openly speculate about is built up by our reading of the text. Think back to the imaginary scenario that opened this chapter. That fictional character met up with you and you imagined your reaction. That was an opening leading out of the closed world of the text in which you first read about or saw that character. It wasn't a part of what you first read about that character over a year ago but it was almost certainly based on things you found out back at that original encounter.

As with many of the debates in this book, there is a need to see all sides of the argument. We want to introduce young readers to a range of characters that they will enjoy reading about. The more personality these characters acquire the better. At the same time, we want to demystify the process of characterisation, making it clear to children what it is in the stories we read that results in our engagement with characters. Going back to Adele Berlin's comments on the cake in the Introduction, we want our readers to see the recipe, not just taste the cake.

IN PRACTICE: THE CONCEPT OF CHARACTER

What these debates show is the way in which readers develop a certain instinctive response to the characters encountered in reading. There is often something about them that causes a reader to regard them as individual personalities and that can invite interpretation and speculation that takes us beyond the story we read. Working with children to identify and discuss the characters in stories places before them one of the main pleasures that can be gained from reading.

In practical terms there are a number of things we can do to develop this idea of what characters are and what readers make of them. In doing so, the learning objectives will be that children learn to:

- understand and use the term 'character';
- remember and recall characters they have encountered in a variety of stories;
- respond creatively to characters they encounter in stories.

The following activities work towards these aims.

USE THE TERM 'CHARACTER'

When you discuss a book with a group of children, use the term 'character'. To take an example, when seeking out a response to Janet and Allan Ahlberg's *Each Peach Pear Plum* (1978), instead of asking 'Who saved Baby Bunting from the river?' ask 'Which characters saved Baby Bunting from the river?' Children who hear the use of the term 'character' will learn how to use it themselves.

KEEP CHARACTER LISTS

During the reading of a book there is much to be gained from keeping a list of characters encountered as the story progresses. The characters can be logged on a chart which then provides a useful way of recapping on the story up to a particular point. The chart can be more than just a list of names; symbols can be developed to indicate information about a character (for example, crowns for royalty, skulls for pirates). Notes can be scribbled that indicate the relationships between characters.

In working with a Year 3 class on the story of Shakespeare's *Twelfth Night* the complexities of the relationships between the various characters led to many different lines peppered with symbols (the chart can look like an Ordnance Survey map when working on this type of story). A list devised in this way enables children to keep track of the characters in a story and can also be referred to at a later date, after a story has been read. Charts for different stories can be built up into a collection of character lists. These can be put on display or bound into book form to provide a catalogue of characters.

MAKE CHARACTERS

Use as many ways as you can to involve children in the process of selecting characters from stories and producing a product that represents them. Faces can be made on paper circles or paper plates, using a range of materials. Characters can be constructed using modelling material, or puppets representing them can be made. This process will mean that children will be called upon to look at the story to find the information that will help them in the production of their chosen character, such as physical characteristics and descriptions of clothing.

ASSEMBLE CHARACTER FRIEZES

Groups of children can be asked to choose a story and paint a background for it. This should be the place in which the story takes place – perhaps an island, a castle, whatever is appropriate – it is the 'setting' (something we shall deal with in Chapter 3). Children can produce cut-out versions of characters to fix on to the background, placing the characters in the setting.

TAKE AN INTEREST IN CHARACTER FIGURES

A popular way in which children can look at and discuss character is through the merchandising of figurines based on characters in current films. I have had classes that have constructed settings for various Disney characters, for example, incorporating their particular attributes and actions. This type of activity can promote a wealth of discussion on the range of characters in a story.

TAKE THEM ELSEWHERE

Don't just discuss characters in the place where the story sets them. Use the idea of a character as an open construct. Readers can be creative. Look at other contexts and ask what they would do there. How would David McKee's *Two Monsters* (1987) behave on the school playground, or what would happen if Tony Ross's *Super Dooper Jezebel* (1988) visited the Queen? Such starter questions can lead to interesting discussion or drama.

CHARACTER TRAITS

What is a particular character like? A character's traits stand outside the time span of the story, underpinning it with an insight into his or her character.

In Chapter 1 we looked at the way in which a story features events added to events. This elementary story by Seymour Chatman progresses through four simple statements.

> (1) Peter fell ill. (2) He died. (3) He had no friends or relatives. (4) Only one person came to his funeral. (page 43)

Chatman points out that there is a *trait* here that underpins the whole of this mini story, namely point 3. This is not an event. In some ways it is outside the events. Diagrammatically, the story could look something like this:

```
                        3
1 — — — — 2 — — — — — — — — — — 4
```

Statements 1, 2 and 4 tell us something that happened. Statement 3 tells us something about Peter.

There is a sense in which the third point, the trait, shouldn't be on the diagram at all. It is a statement within the events about one of the characters in the story. To quote Chatman again:

> Events travel as vectors, 'horizontally' from earlier to later. Traits, on the other hand, extend over the time spans staked out by the events. (page 129)

For children this concept of a trait can be quite challenging yet powerful. The idea that we can piece together things about a character can be both a productive means of reflecting on a story and an engaging way of developing a young reader's experience of character.

IN PRACTICE: CHARACTER TRAITS

The concept of character traits provides a way of examining the impression a reader forms of a particular character. Here again, we have a term that can be introduced and used. The concept can be looked at in a number of ways that will enable the understanding and sharing of such impressions. The following learning objectives underpin work on traits, aiming for children to:

✧ identify and discuss the traits of various characters;
✧ develop the vocabulary with which to express such insights.

The following sections put forward some of the practical ways in which we can develop the idea of character traits.

COLLECTING TRAIT WORDS

Children can discuss the traits of people they know, collecting the words they use and writing them on a chart. It is important to stress that the subject of what they do or have done in the past is to be avoided. Can they think of words that describe the person? This should not be simply a list of adjectives – indeed, the activity can come to a quick standstill if children are taxed with the need to provide such a list – but should also include verbs indicating actions associated with the person and nouns that are important items, people or places that the person would consider special. It is not necessary to be tied to having one-word contributions. Short phrases or sentences can be featured.

A creative way of compiling trait words is to ask the person to lie down on a sheet of wallpaper, draw round the person and cut out his or her shape. The person's character traits can then be written on small notes and affixed to the shape.

TRAITS IN STORIES

The above idea can be switched to the reading of a story. Keep a record of things readers get to know about a character while reading a particular story. This can be an interesting way of keeping a diary on a story being read to the whole class. It can be maintained either by the whole class or by a small group. Early on in the reading of a story, introduce the main characters and ask children to select one each. They can then keep a record of the traits they encounter as the class progresses through the text. This will work well with a short novel that can be read over a week, such as Jan Mark's *The Snow Maze* or Anne Fine's *How to Write Really Badly* (1996).

MATCH TRAITS TO CHARACTERS

This involves working through a list of words you provide, asking which ones apply to people they know. A thesaurus is an excellent resource for this task, providing the most extensive array of personal adjectives. You could put together a list of traits that could apply to teachers (strict, sweet, scruffy, tidy, pugilistic) and see which ones apply to the staff in your school. It can make for an excellent survey of opinion!

TRAITS CHARTS

When you have read to the point in a story where it can be said that most of the characters have been introduced and have started to play a part in the action, a set of charts with a picture of each character at the top can be made. Ask children to write something they have to say about each character on a strip of paper, but to keep it to themselves. Then once everyone in the group or class has written a set of sentences, they can be pasted on to the charts.

Look out for similar and different judgements. I recently did this with a Year 4 class working with the book *Krindlekrax*. A lot of children quickly labelled the bully of the story, Elvis, in similar ways ('He is nasty', 'He is too rough', 'He is a bully to Ruskin'). Opinion was divided over some of the other characters, in particular the monster, Krindlekrax. The traits of Krindlekrax defied simplistic categorisation of the character.

With picture books this activity is sometimes best done when the story has ended, though in a book like McKee's *Not Now, Bernard* our feelings towards Bernard's parents can be formed on the first few pages.

PARADIGM OF TRAITS

Chatman uses the phrase 'paradigm' as a label for the collection of traits that we put together in our reading of a character. This is an interesting term to use. A paradigm is the impression or set of ideas formed on the basis of a set of experiences. The term was originally applied to the history of scientific ideas by the writer Thomas S. Kuhn (1970). There was a time when experience dictated the accepted paradigm that the Earth stood still and the Sun went around it. When astronomers started showing the problems with this paradigm it broke down and shifted to a new paradigm backed up by further experiences.

As readers, we characterise people in a similar way. We all know people who we characterise as 'a really lovely person' or a 'bare-faced liar'. Continuing encounters with these people can do two things. They can either confirm our opinion or alter our opinion. It is the same with story characters. We form opinions that can alter as we continue to read the story. We can also form opinions that alter when we re-read the story. Selden (1989) remarks:

> At any given stage in reading there are always a number of possible ways of building a provisional interpretation of the characters and their situation... Our construction of meaning is likely to be open and provisional at the outset, but to become gradually less open and more definite. (page 124)

In a book like Cave's *Something Else* the central character is different from all the other weird creatures that inhabit his world, and they feel that they are superior to him. When one night another strange creature turns up at his door, greeting him and saying 'You're Something Else and I'm one too', he initially rejects this new character's offer of friendship with the rebuff, 'You're definitely not my sort of Something Else.' He becomes as superior in his mind as those who rejected him. The change in his character comes as the second creature wanders off into the night: 'Something Else' is reminded of the way he has been treated and chases after the new character, inviting him to stay.

In Catherine Fisher's novel *The Snow Walker's Son* (1993) half the novel is spent on the heroine's journey to see Kari, the son of an ice witch locked away and said to be monstrous. The suspense builds up. The reader develops a response to Kari. We hear of the midwife screaming at his birth. When someone encounters Kari we are told: 'The man had changed. His face was pale, his voice quiet.'

When we finally come to the heroine's meeting with Kari there is a complete shattering of our expectations (shattering enough for me not to give it away). One paradigm breaks down and is replaced by another. The alteration in a paradigm is a dynamic part of the reading experience.

IN PRACTICE: PARADIGM OF TRAITS

This is such a dynamic part of our reading that we need to draw children's attention to this process if we are to develop their understanding of character. What we are looking for are the ways in which a story proceeds to confirm or alter our reading of a character. Our objectives are that children will learn to:

✧ understand the way in which our interpretation of characters changes during the reading of a story;

✧ review their opinions of characters during their reading;

✧ identify the changes in the paradigm of traits they formulate for a particular character;

✧ assess why their response to a character changes as the paradigm is reformulated.

The following section provides activities in this vein.

REVIEWING TRAIT CHARTS

If we look at changes we make in our perceptions of characters over time and review the trait charts, we begin to see how open and provisional views of characters alter and become more definite. A character like Boothe in Lesley Howarth's book *Maphead* (1994) seems strangely alien in the opening chapter as he drinks a catshake and learns to use 'natural speech'. As we read on into his search for his mother and, ultimately, for love, we define our reading of this character more clearly.

CHARACTER LINES

It is useful to draw a set of vertical parallel lines on a large piece of paper and chart the perceptions an individual or the class forms of various characters at different stages in the reading of a story. It is interesting because it enables the changes in characters to be placed side by side.

In Cave's *Something Else* the two central characters take turns at being friendly and withdrawn. Their reactions to each other work side by side. In a film like *Toy Story* the point at which Buzz Lightyear gives up in despair is also the point at which the cynical Woody becomes the great encourager. Woody then sinks into despair as Buzz becomes the optimist. The changes in these two characters work in a neat parallel. They criss-cross each other in their optimism and despair.

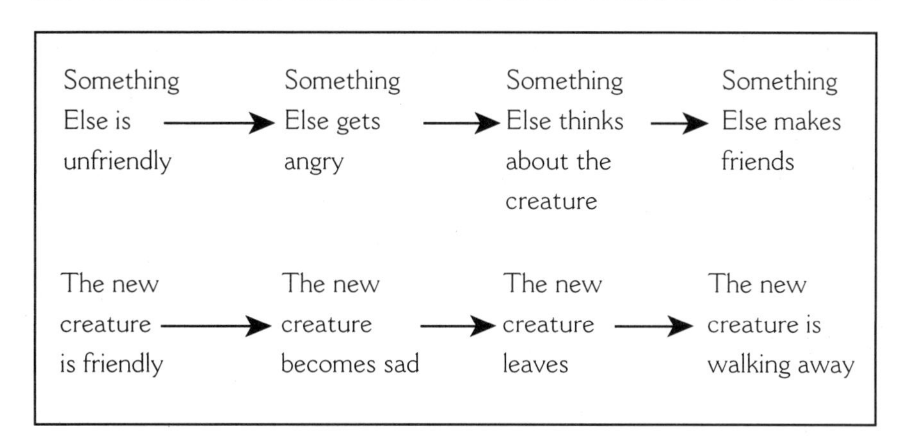

KEEP A DIARY

The earlier activity 'Traits in stories' (page 59) involved children choosing and recording their experience of a particular character during the reading of a story. A diary in the form of a record of how we 'get on' with a particular character over time will show the points at which our response to them changes.

Shorter stories can prove interesting because the character changes can be seen within the brief timescale it takes to read the whole text. Again an excellent example of this is Jan Mark's *The Snow Maze* in which the characters alter considerably within an economically brief amount of text. The story can be read in stages, allowing pauses for each child to record their response to a particular character. These will often alter as the process of paradigm change takes place.

START/END IMPRESSIONS

The impressions of a character formed at the start and at the end of a story can be recorded. Our impressions of the brother and sister in Anthony Browne's *The Tunnel* (1989) alter radically as they are changed by the events of the story.

If the children write three things about a character at the start of a story, then record three things about the same character at the end of a story, they can look at the differences between the impressions. In some cases there will be a clear link between the two of them. (For example, the child who, reading the opening of *The Tunnel*, writes about the brother and sister in the story: 'They don't like each other' and then at the conclusion decides 'They are friends now' will have recorded a significant change in the story.) These changes can be reflected upon by asking why they occurred.

CHARACTERISATION

How do we know whatever we know about a character? Readers develop their understanding of a character through the various methods of characterisation they encounter in the text. This 'make up' of characters produces the text we respond to in interpreting characterisation.

One of the effects of seeing characters as constructs is that it causes us to see how they are constructed. Go back to the character you imagined at the start of this chapter. In playing that scenario most readers will have had some idea of that character encountering them – yet the character is a fictional construct. There are a number of ways in which such characters can be structured so that they can be imagined as a person. The primary distinction to make here is between direct characterisation and indirect characterisation.

DIRECT CHARACTERISATION

Direct characterisation is when we are told something directly in the text, such as in Roald Dahl's *James and the Giant Peach*:

> Their names were Aunt Sponge and Aunt Spiker, and I am sorry to say that they were both really horrible people. They were selfish and lazy and cruel...'

Or as in Dick King-Smith's *The Finger Eater* (1992):

> ...she was as pretty as a picture, looking as though reindeer butter wouldn't melt in her mouth.
>
> She was also a sensible child who paid attention to what her parents told her.

INDIRECT CHARACTERISATION

A lot of the impressions we gain about a character are formed without anyone telling us something directly. This *indirect characterisation* occurs in a number of ways. No one tells us ET is lovable. They don't need to! We just listen to his pleas to 'phone home' and look at the way he makes plants come to life.

Rimmon-Kenan lists some ways in which characterisation can be indirectly communicated to the reader, including:

✧ actions;
✧ speech;
✧ appearance;
✧ environment;
✧ analogy.

It may help to explain each of these indirect forms of characterisation briefly, using examples from children's fiction. We can then look at their implications for reading and responding in the classroom.

ACTIONS

These include habitual actions and single actions that form our impression of a character. So two characters like Aunt Sponge and Aunt Spiker show a cruel consistency. Alternatively, the single action of the thieving performed by the child in Paul Jenning's *The Gizmo* (1994) is introduced with the opening words of the book: 'I have never stolen anything before.'

In Shirley Hughes's *Dogger* a defining moment for the character of Bella is the point at which she gives away a giant teddy bear to redeem her brother's favourite toy. The only characterisation of Foo Foo in the text of Michael Rosen's *Little Rabbit Foo Foo* (1990) is his action of riding through the forest hitting other characters on the head.

SPEECH

This heading can include the speech and thoughts of a character reported in the text. The process of characterisation is added to by the things they say and the things they think.

Part of the success of Philip Ridley's novels lies in his use of speech to maintain strong characterisation. Ridley has a background in scripting film and most of his stories are taken up with dialogue. In *Kaspar and the Glitter* the members of the urban gang that surrounds the menacing King Streetwise each have a distinctive way of addressing Kaspar ('Squire', 'Old Bean', 'Chief', 'Matey') that suits their personality. The inadequacies of the father, Winston, in Ridley's novel *Krindlekrax* are expressed in his two catchphrases 'It's not my fault' and 'Don't interfere'. Anthony Browne's 'Willy the Wimp' (1984) is presented in a similar light: 'When someone knocked into him, he always said, "Oh, I'm sorry!" even when it wasn't his fault.'

APPEARANCE

The appearance of a character has an obvious impact on readers of picture books. One wonders if any of us would remember the wild things half as well as we do if we had never seen Sendak's illustrations. Yet in novels, without the use of illustrations, we are still given a vivid impression of 'the Imperial Princess Margaretta, who dyes her hair blue' (in Susan Price's *The Ghost Drum*, 1987), for example, or '...a little goblin of a man with red cheeks and red whiskers and a red night cap' (in Terry Jones's *Nicobobinus*, 1985).

A character's appearance will be affected by certain aspects of his or her personality or character, such as the dyed blue hair of Princess Margaretta. Others, such as the red whiskers, will be a natural part of the person's appearance. In discussing this aspect of characterisation we need to be cautious. Children can be cruel enough about the appearance of others without our supporting the process.

There are children who will not be helped by the way in which a writer like Hugh Scott depicts the obesity of Anaglypta in *Freddie and the Enormouse* (1989) in such a negative way. It demeans a story that could have been so good when a character is described as cruelly as: 'Plodding slowly in the midst of the rush hour traffic was a large pink blob with a smaller pink blob – cousin Anaglypta's head – on top.'

When looking at aspects of character with children it is worth clarifying the difference between appearances created by characters and those natural to them. For instance, why would anyone dye their hair blue?

ENVIRONMENT

The environments in which characters are depicted can make a significant contribution to our impressions of them. You see this clearly in *A Dark, Dark Tale* by Ruth Brown (1981) in which a cat makes its way through a spooky house. The environment adds substantially to the aura surrounding the prowler.

Once again there is a difference between those features that are within the control of characters and those that are outside their control. The following passage from *A Christmas Carol* (1843) demonstrates how these opposite features work together within the character of Scrooge. Having told us directly that Scrooge is 'a squeezing, wrenching, grasping, scraping, clutching, covetous old sinner!', Dickens goes on to describe the frozen conditions in which he works and to which he subjects his employee:

> ...old Scrooge sat busy in his counting-house. It was cold, bleak, biting weather: foggy withal: and he could hear the people in the court outside, go wheezing up and down... The door of Scrooge's counting-house was open that he might keep an eye upon his clerk, who in a dismal little cell beyond, a sort of tank, was copying letters. Scrooge had a very small fire, but the clerk's fire was so very much smaller that it looked like one coal.

There is a clear purpose to the door being kept open. Scrooge keeps his clerk in 'a sort of tank'. The clerk's fire is 'so very much smaller'. These are parts of the environment but they are enabling our understanding of the character of Scrooge to form.

ANALOGY

Impressions of a character can be reinforced by places or people depicted in the same text, who stand alongside them and who work with or in contrast to them. The depiction of the landscape, for example, can give the reader some sense of a character's mood. The difference between one character and another can define both more fully. Rimmon-Kenan gives the example of the good character, Cordelia, who stands in stark contrast to her two greedy sisters in the opening scene of Shakespeare's *King Lear*.

Roald Dahl puts this to full use in *Charlie and the Chocolate Factory* (1967) when the five children who are shown around the chocolate factory act as foils that set off the character of Charlie.

IN PRACTICE: CHARACTERISATION

The objectives we could set ourselves in utilising this analysis of characterisation in the classroom include the aims that children learn to:

✧ understand the ways in which characterisation can take place in a text;

✧ identify the main processes of characterisation at work in certain texts;

✧ use this understanding to raise and answer questions about characterisation in stories;

✧ use this understanding of characterisation in the stories they write.

Understanding the constituent elements of characterisation can, in itself, alter our reading to and with children. It can enable us as teachers to:

✧ point out and stress significant aspects of characterisation as we read to children;

✧ set an agenda for the questions we ask children about the texts they read or have read to them;

✧ re-read significant parts of a text in which we are conscious of characterisation taking place;

✧ enjoy and develop our own reading of children's literature, as we reflect on some of the excellent processes of characterisation in a text.

The following activities show some specific ways in which we can work with children on the process of characterisation.

PLOT BOX FOR CHARACTERISATION

Characterisation can play a part in children's story writing by encouraging them to use the plot box idea from chapter 1 (see page 35). For example, a child who writes 'There was a wicked wizard' can be asked to describe the wizard's appearance or to insert a conversation between the wizard and a victim.

COLLECTING CHARACTERISATION

It is a good idea to gather together the hints and descriptions in a story to collect the things that characterise a character, possibly keeping a chart on some characters, as in the character lines described earlier. This would have the added dimension of locating the things that changed a character as we progressed through the narrative.

QUESTIONNAIRES

A simple questionnaire can set before a reader some questions about characters encountered in reading, such as: What do they do? What do they say? What do they look like? Where do they live?

MATCHING WORDS

Two sets of cards can be made, one with the names of characters, the other with something said by each of them. This may be a refrain, such as Big Bear's question 'Can't you sleep, Little Bear?' in the Martin Waddell book of the same name (1988). It can be a sentence or phrase said once but memorable thereafter. A good example of this is when Grandfather interrupts Lily listening to the sea in Dyan Sheldon and Gary Blythe's *The Whales' Song* with the order 'Enough of this foolishness'; he only says it once in the whole story but it is powerfully typical of his character.

The cards can then be used for matching activities. The children are given the deck and they have to match card to card. I have used one set of cards with the catchphrases of different characters on them, held up to teams of children who have to answer 'Who said this?' (Something interesting I noticed was that they read it word for word, then repeated it in the tone or voice of that character before answering.) Stories like those by Philip Ridley, referred to earlier in the section on speech (page 66) provide a good resource for this particular activity.

CAUSALITY

As noted above, set of phrases or sentences that describe a character in a story can be compiled, then the ones that the character has control over separated from the ones over which he does not have control. As we saw when we looked at appearance and environment, there is a grey area that divides these and it can result in some fascinating subject matter for debate. For example, Kathryn Cave's character 'Something Else' is ostracised from the other creatures in the story and is introduced with the words:

> On a windy hill
> alone
> with nothing to be friends with
> lived Something Else.

This prompts the question: is he alone because he lives up there or does he live alone on the hill because no one wants his company?

The underlying idea in this activity is the requirement to distinguish between things a character could or couldn't change about his or her characterisation. It is a complex distinction but an important one.

COMPARE AND CONTRAST

One of the ways in which we can work with children on this idea of 'reinforcement by analogy' is by comparing two characters that stand alongside each other in a story. This is best done using two characters that make for an interesting comparison, as in the following example which shows a set of comparisons made between two characters from Ridley's *Krindlekrax*.

Ruskin	Elvis
No friends	Friends with Sparky
Small and puny	Really strong – lots of muscles
Cares for people	Doesn't treat people well
Good actor	Can't act
Is not picked for the play	Is picked for the play

CHARACTER ROLES

If we accept that there is a lot more to characters than their actions we are still bound to maintain the importance of their function within the plot. This will involve looking at what they do and how far the actions of different characters make up the full story.

As we have seen earlier, with their concentration on the way the action of stories is structured, a number of structuralist theorists have concentrated on how the actions of a character are moulded by the role he or she plays in the plot. This brings us back to the functional idea that characters are what they do. This sort of approach has looked at some of the common roles we find in any narrative and the way they interrelate.

In his study of *The Morphology of the Folk Tale*, Vladimir Propp ascribes a limited set of types to the characters in such stories. They include the actions of a villain, a donor, a helper, a sought-after person (and her father), a dispatcher, a hero and a false hero. Propp was able to produce this list of roles after analysing over a hundred fairy tales.

A.J. Greimas (1983) takes this analysis a step further by working with six *actants*: roles that can be played within a narrative. He suggests that the actions of these actants are like the ways grammatical features, such as subject and object, work at a deeper level in a sentence. It may be 'I ate a piece of toast' or 'Nelson Mandela defeated apartheid'. Different words play the role of the subject ('I...'/'Nelson Mandela...') and object ('a piece of toast...'/'apartheid...') but there are a small number of other roles in sentences. It is the words that fill these roles that change.

Greimas builds upon the subject/object structure and outlines three pairs of actants: subject–object; sender–receiver; helper–opponent. He devised a diagram representing the ways in which different actants interrelate in a story.

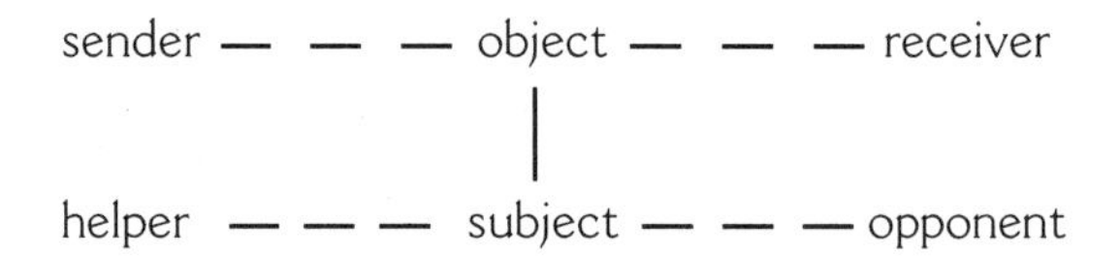

The sender is the one who wants the object to get to the receiver. The subject is the one who takes that object, assisted by the helper and hindered by the opponent. These actants become specific actors in a particular story.

In *Little Red Riding Hood*, the mother acts as sender sending food, the object, to Grandma, the receiver. Little Red Riding Hood is the subject who takes the food. The wolf acts as an opponent, trying to eat them all, but they are eventually helped by the woodcutter who acts as helper and chops open the wolf.

mother — — — — — — — food — — — — Grandma

|

woodcutter — — Little Red Riding Hood — — wolf

In a quest story like Ende's *The Neverending Story* (1983) Atreyu (subject) is sent by the childlike Empress (sender) to bring Bastian (object) to Fantastica (receiver), helped in his mission by characters such as the Luckdragon and his horse Artax (helpers) while being opposed by characters such as Ygramul and Gmork (opponents), as well as by an inanimate object, 'The Nothing' (opponent), that threatens to destroy Fantastica.

In a James Bond film the subject, James Bond, is sent by 'M' (sender) with a mission to take something (the object) to a contact in some exotic location (receiver). Along the way he is backed up by 'Q' (a helper) and hindered by the villain (opponent).

The model also works well with a number of popular television cartoon stories. To varying degrees, children can identify the roles in such series.

Sometimes the roles of two actants can be fulfilled by the same actor, as when the subject is sending the object or when the subject sets out in pursuit of an object he or she will receive. At this point it would be worth thinking through some simple storylines you are familiar with and figuring out how those actants feature within them. Sometimes the model works smoothly, sometimes there are hitches, but it provides a set of axes along which we can place the characters in most of the stories we read.

IN PRACTICE: ROLES

Considering the roles various actants play in the workings of a story can enrich a young reader's understanding of character. In a way it's like being familiar with the grammar of language – understanding how sentences are structured helps us to speak and write. In the same way the reader's competence is enhanced by the expectations and understanding of this deep story grammar structuring the way in which a story works. I can think of a four-year-old who had seen the films *James and the Giant Peach* and *The Hunchback of Notre Dame* and identified the role of the villain in both, explaining that 'Judge Frollo is like Aunt Spiker'. He had drawn a clear parallel between the villains of the two films.

This model can provide the teacher with a new insight into the workings of stories. The type of analysis it promulgates is also a tool for analysis of character role in the classroom. The activities suggested below support the following learning objectives. Children should learn to:

✧ understand the major roles common to many stories;
✧ match characters in stories they encounter to these roles;
✧ investigate how a character suits a particular role as the story progresses.

This familiarity with the types of character encountered in reading can be promoted using activities such as the ones outlined below.

CHARACTER GRID

Story	Heroine or Hero	What is the object?	Villain(s)	Helper(s)	Receives good things
Cinderella	Cinderella	marriage	Ugly sisters	Fairy godmother	Prince Charming
Little Red Riding Hood	Little Red Riding Hood	to deliver food	Wolf	Woodcutter	Grandma
The Lion King	Simba	to become king	Scar	Nala Rafiki	Simba Pride Rock animals

In the above grid the actantial roles have been adapted to form the horizontal axis. Various stories can be placed along the vertical axis by the teacher or the child. The task then is to complete the grid, deciding which characters assume various roles in the stories.

You can vary the horizontal grid depending on the age of the children. The titles Greimas uses are not the most helpful. Terms such as 'heroine/hero' and 'villain' may best describe the role to children. 'Object' can be qualified with a note in brackets: (what the story is all about), which doesn't present the idea in its full complexity but this can be acquired by working with the model on the story concerned. In using this model we need to give some understanding of the object as that which is transferred or sought after in the story. Also, differentiating between terms such as 'helper' and 'subject' can be difficult, as they are so often linked and work together.

GOOD/BAD/IN THE MIDDLE

Younger children can start their exploration of character roles by picking out the characters that are good and the ones that are bad. In stories like Catherine Storr's *Clever Polly and the Stupid Wolf* (1980) it is straightforward, but it is interesting to see where they place characters like the wild things in *Where the Wild Things Are* or the goody goody Jezebel in Tony Ross's *Super Dooper Jezebel*. These more anarchic heroes and roguish villains can cause some debate.

I once worked with a Key Stage 2 class looking at an abridged version of Shakespeare's *The Tempest*. By the end of Act 1 they were quite clear Prospero was 'a baddie' for colonising Caliban's island (a view they share with a number of contemporary critics of the play!).

REVIEWING A GRID

One trick a story can play on us is to make the reader pigeon-hole a character prematurely. We are given the impression the character is a villain only to find, as we read on, that he or she is not. As a teenager, I read many thrillers by Edgar Wallace. This technique was a favourite ploy of his, leading the reader to believe that 'the sinister man' was a villain until he came up trumps and saved the day in the closing pages (Wallace's *The Sinister Man*, 1924).

Similarly, in the children's novel *Wivern Winter* (1992) by Toby Forward, from our first meeting with Felicity Aylmer she is presented as sinister. Under an illustration that presents her looking unnerving there is this description:

> A second pair of eyes watched the children. Sharp eyes in a keen face... And these eyes had caught the small movement in the upper window of Wivern Manor.
>
> 'There's someone in there,' she said to Shakti. 'They've arrived.'
>
> Shakti slithered round Felicity Aylmer's neck and slid through her hands, his shiny scales warm to her touch.

Subtly, we are given hints. The sharp eyes, the pet snake and the fact that she surreptitiously watches the children, our heroes. It causes many children to suspect her on first encounter and she remains a sinister figure. But as the story progresses we find she is on the side of the children and is out to tackle the evil forces that lurk in Wivern Manor.

In the children's film *Labyrinth* the helper is a goblin called Hoggle who has been sent by the goblin king (opponent) to lead the heroine (or subject) astray. But there is a constant conflict between his love for the heroine and his fear of the goblin king, and neither the viewer nor, for that matter, Hoggle himself, is sure until the very end whose side he is really on.

It can be interesting to see how a character grid evolves during our reading of a story. The villain becomes a heroine. The hero gives up and the one whom we thought would be just a trusty helper turns out to be the one who saves the day. The goblin, Rumpelstiltskin in the Brothers Grimm fairy tale initially appears as a helper but becomes a villain, demonstrating that roles can be altered as the characters develop.

ROLE QUIZ

Once this type of character analysis has been applied to a number of stories, the class should have a comprehensive list of the characters who take on the different roles in a range of stories. These lists can furnish a quiz based around questions such as 'Who is the villain in *The Lion, the Witch and the Wardrobe*?' and 'In the film version of *Aladdin*, what is his helper called?' This will involve children searching for the name in their minds even though they will have been engrossed in the book or film at an earlier stage.

TRACING A CHARACTER'S ROLE

When a story has ended you can unravel the different points in the story in which a certain character was crucial. When a group of characters cluster together in a story they will often bring something necessary to the narrative. In the old Russian folk tale *The Flying Ship* the hero is given a flying ship to take to the Czar with the instruction that he must offer a lift on board to any who require it. He then collects a motley collection of characters (including a man with incredible ears and a man with a leg tied behind his back). When he reaches the Czar's palace and the Czar starts setting him impossible challenges the abilities of his passengers prove essential ('Ears' hears the Czar plotting, 'Leg tied' can run fast enough to complete one of the impossible challenges).

The idea of a set of characters contributing their own special abilities to a task is common in quest stories. Stories such as the BBC series *Through the Dragon's Eye* (Russell and Russell, 1989) contain a trio of children, each of whom brings their own particular qualities to the quest they embark on. A number of television adventures involve a set of characters trekking round the universe or through various locations. These individuals contribute certain attributes that support the rest of the group. On completing such stories it is worth tracing back particular characters' roles in the tale, asking:

- Where did they come in?
- What did they do?
- What if they hadn't been in the story?
- What happened to them in the end?

CONCLUSION

Let us return briefly to the mini-debates earlier in the chapter between characters being or doing and the extent to which they are open or closed constructs, which underpin all that we have looked at in this chapter. Writing about the character of Sarrasine in Balzac's story of the same name, Roland Barthes (1990) writes:

> We occasionally speak of Sarrasine as though he existed, as though he had a future, an unconscious, a soul; however what we are talking about is his *figure* (an impersonal network of symbols combined under the proper name 'Sarrasine'), not his *person*... (page 94)

This chapter has enabled us to look at such impersonal networks of symbols. In a way, when we read or watch a story, that is all there is to our encounter with the characters, and this apparent piece of relegation of character is, in fact, one of the best things about stories. Seeing character as a network of symbols gives us an insight into their workings that can not only enhance our appreciation but also excite our reading and stimulate our creativity.

CHAPTER 3

SETTING

I have an attic full of cardboard. Boxes of different shapes and sizes clutter the space. They are elaborate constructions, taped, tied or glued together, that make up the various settings that have struck a chord with the children during the reading of a story or a trip to the cinema. I have the farm from *The Sheep-Pig*, Luke Skywalker's base from *Star Wars*... the list goes on. Each construction is evidence of the way in which the setting can play an important role in a story. In the same way that a particular character can remain the most memorable feature of a story, it is also possible for the setting to have a lingering effect. As Toolan (1988) states in his study of the setting of stories:

> ...though less fundamentally essential to narrative than event and character... the establishment of an identifiable setting is a strong psychological preference in most readers. We like, in our reading of narratives, to know where we are, and look for clear spatiotemporal indications of just where and when a thing happened. (page 103)

The setting of a story can evoke a series of powerful images in the reader's imagination. However, there are varying degrees to which the setting has an impact on the action or the characters of a story. Sometimes there is a sense in which characters and events are essential to stories while the setting can be filled in by the reader or listener. Seymour Chatman points out that:

> Characters are only there, on the scene, when their presence is announced or strongly implied. But we can always 'fill in', so to speak, whatever is needful to authenticate a setting. (page 141)

So it is possible to read the story of *Jack and the Beanstalk* without requiring a description of Jack's house, the road to market or the giant's castle. This is because the reader can fill in such settings, using his or her own imagination. Toolan cites the example of a fable as a story which has no specific setting. In such tales it is not needed. However, this should not lead to a dismissal of setting as unimportant but rather to a recognition that setting can have varying importance in stories. Such a conclusion also leads to an understanding that when setting becomes important in a story the effect can be highly significant. As Powell (1993) notes:

> Some settings (such as Camelot, the Garden of Eden, or the land of Oz) become so clearly entrenched in the mind of the reader that they, like memorable characters, take on a life of their own. (page 70)

What we have here is a scale. At one end of the scale we could place the fable, in which the setting is of practically no significance. At the other we may place a story like Frances Hodgson Burnett's *The Secret Garden* (1911) in which the setting is crucial.

EXISTENTS

Conventionally, most people would think of a simple distinction between the setting and the characters. The setting may be thought of as like a theatre set in which the backdrop is painted, furniture is laid out and so on. The character then steps on to this platform. However, the distinction is not quite so clear cut. For example, picture the setting of a cocktail party. Such a setting is composed of people. The room in which the party takes place is not so relevant. The setting is made up of a particular group of people involved in a particular social situation. They may be chattering in the background. They are not really performing a role as characters; they could be seen rather as the backdrop of the story.

The connection between character and setting can be seen in the analysis of narrative structure outlined by Seymour Chatman. Chatman draws a distinction between the *events* and *existents* in a story. In the former category he classes the events that make up the plot of the story, so in the case of Sendak's *Where the Wild Things Are* this would include an event such as the boy visiting a land full of monsters. In the latter category he places two sub-classes of existents, one being characters, the other setting. Again, to take *Where the Wild Things Are* as an example, the existents would be characters, such as the wild things and Max, and the setting of the land of the wild things.

Chatman makes the point that the demarcation between character and setting is not a clear-cut division. It is more of a continuum. The distinction between character and setting is one of degree. To return to my earlier example, if at the cocktail party one of the guests does something embarrassing then there is a sense in which they have come out of the backdrop and taken on an element of characterisation.

SETTING: MOOD, ACTION AND LOCATION

The significance of setting can be seen in the functions it performs in the story. The three principal functions of setting are: the contribution it can make to the mood of a story, the part it can play in the action of a story and the way in which it can locate a story in a historical and geographical location.

SETTING AND MOOD

Chatman highlights the contribution to mood as the 'normal and perhaps principal function of setting'. There is a sense in which a setting can be in keeping with the characters or the events in the story. This analogous function can be seen in the way in which the misery of the setting in Philip Ridley's *Dakota of the White Flats* (1989) reinforces the misery of the characters. The story presents characters whose lives are dogged by the past and who live in a run-down, unnamed urban landscape. Their one avenue of escapism is to read the novels of a

romantic author who, incidentally, lives in an expensive fortress on an island in the middle of the river that runs behind their supermarket. The writer lives apart from the miserable lives of his readers.

Such a setting can enhance the mood that influences the reader's understanding of characters and the situation in which they find themselves. In the previous chapter on characterisation a note of caution is placed on linking characters with their environment. It needs to be borne in mind that there is sometimes a direct causal link between characters and their setting, and at other times they have little or no influence over the setting. Characters may create their setting. They may also be created by their setting. The character 'Something Else' in Kathryn Cave's story lives on a lonely hillside because the other creatures ostracise him – it is not his choice – whereas the cold environment in which Scrooge chooses to work in Dickens' *A Christmas Carol* and to which he subjects his employee is something he could easily afford to change (he 'causes' the setting and it tells us something about his character).

SETTING AND ACTION

Settings can present obstacles to characters, provide advantages and alter the course of events. Throughout the action of a story the characters can interact with the setting. For example, the children on their quest in Rosen's *We're Going on a Bear Hunt* encounter obstacle after obstacle and have to wade through rivers and squelch through mud. In Ian Beck's story of *Tom and the Island of Dinosaurs* (1995) events are dominated first by the threat and then by the eruption of the island's volcano. In both these examples the setting has a direct effect on the action of the story.

It isn't just characters who can play a part in the events of a story. Greimas's actantial model introduces the role of the helper. In *Rosie's Walk* by Pat Hutchins it is the farmyard that comes to the help of Rosie the hen. Each of the fox's efforts to catch Rosie are frustrated by various props scattered around the farmyard, such as the pond he falls into and the flour that buries him. Various parts of the setting are playing a part in the story.

The interaction between setting and the events of the story is most vividly seen in the quest story. The characters in *Through the Dragon's Eye* by Russell and Russell and in *The Neverending Story* by Ende undertake a journey. They are opposed by other characters but they also face challenges built into the setting. The gulf that the characters must cross to continue a journey, the snowstorm in which one of the characters is separated from the rest of the band – such settings create events in a story. This placing of obstacles throughout a setting is also an essential part of adventure game stories, in which the reader charts a course past the various obstacles.

SETTING AND LOCATION

While taking Chatman's point that the reader can fill in details of a setting that are not presented in a story, it must also be noted that setting can provide the reader with details essential to an understanding of the story. When the children in *The Lion, the Witch and the Wardrobe* step through a piece of furniture into a magic land, the clear implication is that they are walking beyond the familiar into the magical. In such cases setting can define the boundaries of a story, indicating the conventions that will prevail. For example, as Toby steps through the mirror in Anthony Browne's picture book *Through The Magic Mirror* (1976) he enters a place where, in illustration after illustration, conventions are overturned. This can have an important link to the genre of the story. In Browne's *The Tunnel*, a down-to-earth, realistic story of brother and sister conflict becomes a fantasy story as the children follow a tunnel to an enchanted forest. Beverly Naidoo's powerful tale *Journey to Jo'burg: A South African Story* (1985) opens with two pages and a map that set the story in the South Africa of apartheid. Without that locative introduction the reader could struggle to root the events that follow in context.

IN PRACTICE: SETTING

Setting is a feature of the text that requires the activity of the teacher if the child is to take an interest in it. As readers we are often keen to know who is doing what. I'm sure I am not the only reader who has skipped a nineteenth-century author's descriptions of a blasted heath because I want to get down to what happens on the heath. However, skipping such descriptive texts is a mistake. For the reader who is prepared to stop and dwell on the descriptions there can often be a distinct pleasure. Involving children in working on the settings of stories will fulfil the following learning objectives. Children should learn to:

✧ appreciate the various settings in which a story can be set;

✧ recognise some of the features that contribute to an impression of setting;

✧ evaluate the effect various settings have on the stories in which they are depicted.

The following activities are structured around these learning objectives.

VARIETY

Children can keep a catalogue of the various settings they encounter in their own reading or watching of stories. It can be an individual effort but there are advantages to a catalogue made by the whole class. A catalogue built up over a period of a few weeks, with the name of the type of setting and a brief description, can serve to illustrate the variety of places that can be depicted in stories. It can also serve as a stimulus in creative writing. Very often the child who is going through the 'I don't know what to write' block can be stimulated by the suggestion of a setting. A pirate ship or a creepy house, for example, lend themselves to creative writing.

LIST FIVE

One way of starting the above catalogue is to ask every child to make their own independent list of five favourite locations for the setting of a story. The various lists can then be collated on to one big list. If a suggestion is mentioned a second time, a tick is placed against its name. Certain settings will receive a number of ticks, particularly if a craze for a current film or television series causes it to appear on a large number of personal lists.

THE LANGUAGE OF SETTING

Texts can be analysed to find within them the various words and phrases that build up a picture of the setting. In shorter picture books such setting descriptions may be limited. This makes them an excellent resource for children to trawl through in search of the language of setting. Lists can be compiled of how the various settings are presented. Such an activity will also draw on the children's descriptive language as they formulate ways of listing their own description of the setting as it appears in illustrated form.

COMPARISON

Earlier it was suggested that two characters in the same story can be compared and contrasted. This can be particularly pronounced in the different locations inside a story but it can also be interesting to compare two locations from different stories. One way of doing this is to have two small groups of equal number with each group examining the setting of separate stories. It helps if the book is new to the class but this is not essential for the activity. The story should be short enough to be read in under ten minutes.

Having read the story, each group has to think of some important things they could tell the other group about their particular setting. The two groups then confer by comparing settings. For example, one of the things the first group may notice about their setting is 'This was a magical place'. The second group offers the comparison with their story, which may share that particular feature or not. It may share it in part, for example 'It wasn't magical at first but it got to be like that.'

After swapping five comparisons each, the groups can list

them as a record of their findings. It is important in this final stage of the activity to give each group enough time to read the other group's story.

MAPPING

Some stories contain maps in the opening pages. Quest stories, such as J.R.R. Tolkien's *The Hobbit* (1937) and C.S. Lewis's *Prince Caspian* (1951) open with a map that presents their magical setting. More realistic settings are depicted in the opening maps of books like Robert Leeson's *The Third Class Genie* (1975) or the map of Alton Towers that opens Helen Cresswell's *The Watchers* (1993). Such maps can be copied on a larger scale and followed during the reading of a story. Other stories that don't have such maps can provide a stimulus for children to produce their own versions. A list of locations visited in a story such as Gibson's *Ellis and the Hummick* (1989), a quest that lacks a map, can be used to produce a map of the places visited. These can be embellished with dire warnings and notes about events that took place at the various locations.

It isn't just novels that can include illustrations mapping out their settings. Picture books such as Hutchins's *Rosie's Walk* and Janet and Allan Ahlberg's *Each Peach Pear Plum* open with double-page spreads that map out their settings. Here again, the routes the stories take can be traced on maps.

LOCATING THE LOCATION

Stories can be located in various temporal and geographical settings. The class can produce a timeline or use a world map to locate the stories they encounter. There is in fact a paucity of quality books from a variety of historical settings, particularly among material aimed at younger readers. However, the net can be widened beyond books – varied locations can be found in children's cartoon films and television programmes. A quick glance over a range of Disney releases will present a variety of locations, from the Agrabah of the Arabian Nights in *Aladdin* to Victor Hugo's Paris in *The Hunchback of Notre Dame*. Children can be shown that although such stories may be fictional they often draw on settings that have both a historical and a geographical location.

CREATING SETTINGS

Settings lend themselves to creative depiction. In the previous chapter an activity is suggested in which children create a large picture of a setting for a story against which the characters are depicted (page 56). These can be specific, as in the case of the setting of a particular story. But children also take with enthusiasm to the idea of producing a type of setting that is not tied to one story, and can collect a range of ideas from a variety of stories that utilise such settings.

Activities in which children reproduce a setting from a story or devise a setting for a story involve them in replicating the sorts of features that make up the setting. As well as pictures, models of locations can be produced. A box with a side cut away can be painted and the inside turned into the setting for a particular character or set of characters, such as Mr Tumnus's house from *The Lion, the Witch and the Wardrobe*. There is something about the space of a box that can stimulate the imagination. Children who are asked to produce a setting inside a box will often produce some incredibly intricate props. Throughout this process there can be a use of story texts to suggest items that could be incorporated into the setting.

The idea of story setting can also stimulate some interesting locations with which to structure a play area. The pirate cave, the magician's kitchen or the spaceship can provide a setting in which children are engaging in the excitement evoked by a particular story setting.

TEACHER-MADE MAPS

As a teacher, one of the activities I have enjoyed is that of devising maps of settings in which children can locate their own stories. It gives the teacher an opportunity to produce a magic land or island that draws on the stock of locations and contains various characters built up through all the experience of reading children's literature. So an island could have a shore where the wild things live, for example; further inland there could be a chocolate factory or the home of a goblin.

A map on a large sheet of paper showing various locations can be an enormous stimulus to children who will want to add locations themselves or to use the ones already on the map in their story writing. The main advantage of the use of such maps is they allow the teacher to play to the tastes of the class. Favourite locations and characters can be placed on the map, allowing children to pick and mix a route through this land and imaginatively interact with whoever they meet on the way.

CONCLUSION

While recognising the varying degree to which setting can matter in a story, it is also important to remember that it has the potential to become the most memorable existent from a story. The images and effects such settings can present in stories can, as Powell points out, make them just as memorable as the characters in that they take on a life of their own. An evocative depiction of setting can be found in some comments made by Philip Ridley (in Hunt, 1994) about the East End setting in which he grew up, a setting that has featured so prominently in his stories. It shows the sort of feeling that he, as a writer, wraps up in the settings in his stories:

> ...the most common playground for East End children was the bomb site, which was also a rubbish dump. There was a huge one just opposite the house where I grew up... I can still recall the smell of those places in summer, the powerful weeds struggling through the wreckage, and the magic of finding a ladybird or a butterfly... This sort of scenery breeds its own mythology: a car can become a chariot, a sewer a dungeon, a disused factory a castle. (page 17)

CHAPTER 4

NARRATION

Most teachers will have had the experience of the 'big bang playground problem'. This is the term I apply to the task of dealing with a playground fight or bust-up. It works like this. A verbal or physical fracas occurs, the complaint is brought to the teacher and the investigation begins. No individual ever admits to having started the problem. Child A will always blame child B who 'swore at me'. Child B then protests that Child A pushed in the line. Child A says that this is correct but puts it all down to Child B pushing in before them. If this continues, the teacher is facing a problem which, like the 'Big Bang' that started off the universe, has its origins way back in time and, as with the 'Big Bang', nobody is really sure what actually happened.

It is interesting to reflect that such playground incidents, as well as being irritating, also demonstrate an important distinction in narrative theory. The account of the incident is separated from the actual bust-up. As a teacher, it is much easier to deal with issues that arise right in front of you than issues that arose at another time and in another place related to you in a narrative account of what happened. The problem is that, in dealing with the latter, you are reliant on the narration of events for an insight into what actually happened.

This chapter is concerned with that process of narrating events. Having looked at the events that make up the plot of a story, and at the characters involved in events and the setting of the story, this chapter shifts from the content of the narrative, the story, to the actual narrating of the content. This distinction between story and narrative may seem an odd one. However, it opens up a host of considerations about the narrative voice present in all texts. It is a complex distinction that takes us to the historic origin of structuralist theory in the work of Ferdinand de Saussure.

STORY AND NARRATIVE

Structuralist theory has built upon the work of the linguist Ferdinand de Saussure. Originally published in 1915, Saussure's *Course in General Linguistics* provides a number of ideas and terms that have become a bedrock for structuralist theory. One of the basic concepts Saussure presents is his explanation of the linguistic *sign*. According to Saussure a sign is made up of two elements, the *signified* and the *signifier*. The signified and signifier work hand in hand in the process of *signification*. Look at this sign:

It immediately means something. The sign evokes an abstract concept in the reader's mind of a cup or mug containing a drink. The reader may or may not like the drink itself. It could invoke the idea of a jar of a favourite brand in granule form or a filter machine. It may prompt you to go and make one. The marks on the page make up the signifier. The concept it invokes is the signified. When the children in the playground run up shouting, 'Fight, fight!' the shout is the signifier, the concept it invokes in your mind is the signified. You don't need to see the fight itself to have an abstract idea of what the children are referring to. That abstract idea may be an amalgam of years of experience of playground fights. The sign does its job when the sound image (signifier) conjures up the concept (signified).

Gerard Genette draws on the terms signifier and signified to distinguish between the story and its narrative. He sees story as the content, the set of events (see Chapter 1), describing this content of a narrative as the:

> ...actions and situations taken in themselves, without regard to the medium, linguistic or other, through which knowledge of that totality comes to us... (page 25)

The story, in Genette's terms, is the subject matter of the narrative. Genette points out that this content is the signified. Genette then reserves the use of the term *narrative* for 'the signifier, statement, discourse or narrative text itself' (page 27).

In this chapter we will follow Genette's use of the term narrative to denote:

> the narrative statement, the oral or written discourse that undertakes to tell of an event or a series of events...
> (page 25)

So the narrative is the 'telling' of the story.

To return to the example of the playground scuffle, one set of events has taken place. But it is not uncommon for there to be several variant versions of the one set of events, some omitting crucial details, others putting a particular 'spin' on the events. The events themselves undergo a process of narration. The same set of events, the story, becomes the version the teacher has to work with, the narrative.

This distinction highlights the significance of the process of narration. Looking at the ways in which the story is encoded in a narrative involves looking at the role of the narrator, the point of view from which the story is told and the way language is used in the narrating. There is the story that is told and there is the narrative that does the telling.

AUTHOR AND NARRATOR, READER AND NARRATEE

The narrator is not the author. They are different figures in the narrative transaction. When Paul Jennings starts a story like *The Gizmo* with the central character Stephen stating, 'I have never stolen anything before', the one who declares he has never stolen before is the narrator (Stephen), not the author (Jennings). Although many authors openly identify with the characters they create and often draw on their own experience when devising the experiences of the narrators of their stories the two are distinct. In addition to the narrator and the author, there are two other participants in this process of narration. There is the real reader (in the classroom context this can also denote the person who listens to the reading) and the 'narratee', who is the recipient of the narrative as referred to by the text. These participants in the narrative process can be represented diagrammatically:

Author — — — Narrator — — — Narratee — — — Reader

The narrator and the narratee may be clearly designated in the text. In the Shirley Hughes story *Sea Singing* (1993) the narrator is a young girl who recalls her stay with an artist, Morag, in a house beside the sea. When, within this story, Morag tells the girl the story of the selkie bride, a new relationship is present. Now Morag is the narrator and the girl becomes a narratee. The illustration in the picture book shows her sitting, listening to the story.

In Italo Calvino's *If on a Winter's Night a Traveller* (1981) the narratee is addressed directly in the opening words:

> You are about to begin reading Italo Calvino's new novel... Let the world around you fade. Best to close the door; the TV is always on in the next room. Tell the others right away, 'No, I don't want to watch TV!' (page 3)

The real reader may be sitting outside, without a television near, but the narrator is addressing the narratee, the text's version of the one being addressed.

However, the narratee is not always referred to so explicitly. In Hughes's *Alfie Gets in First*, Alfie runs up the steps into the house ahead of Mum. The narrator says:

> Mum put the shopping down in the hall and went back down the steps to lift Annie Rose out of her push-chair. But what do you think Alfie did then?

The question is addressed to a narratee. The role of a participant who receives the text is written into the story.

Another example of the narrator addressing the narratee can be found in Roald Dahl's *The Witches* (1983). The opening 'Note about witches' gives the following warning about a witch:

> She might be the lady with the dazzling smile who offered you a sweet from a white paper bag in the street before lunch.
> She might even – and this will make you jump – she might even be your lovely school-teacher who is reading these words to you at this very moment.

The text addresses someone, assuming something about them and about the context in which they are reading. It assumes that the story will be read to a class in a primary school. It also assumes that the teacher will be female. When I read the story to my class it was quite clear that we, as readers, were distinct from the narratees addressed by the narrator!

Narrators and narratees are inscribed in the text. The narrator says 'I have never stolen anything before' (Jennings). The narratee is asked 'What do you think Alfie did then?' (Hughes). The other participants are outside the text. The diagram can be altered to show the scope of the narrative text.

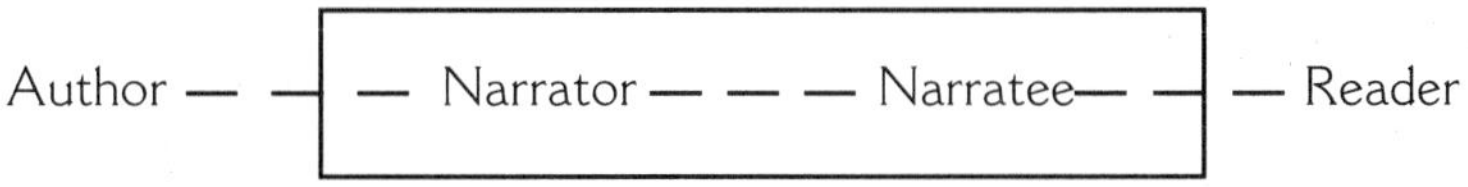

Author — | — Narrator — — — Narratee— | — Reader

The box delineates the narrative text. The real author and the real reader are outside the text. Whatever we know about the real author is a matter of their history or biography. You cannot assume that there is any common ground between the author and the narrator. A writer like Morris Gleitzmann writes in a style that is personal and in touch with the feelings of a child. It would be tempting to assume the text is putting the reader in touch with the experiences of the author. However, Gleitzmann (1994) told *Books for Keeps* magazine (Hunt, 1994):

> 'I've never been able to reflect my own childhood experiences as a writer... My characters come from me as I am now: part of me is an 11-year-old...'

Common ground can only ever be established through knowing something about the author, not from the narrative text itself. Similarly, the reader lies outside the text. When the voice on *Watch with Mother* narrated Andy Pandy's exploits and asked questions such as 'Well, children, can you see where Teddy is hiding?' the narrator was referring to a narratee, the 'children' who would answer the question. But, as individual viewers, we remained outside the text.

THE NARRATOR

The distinction is often made between texts told in the first person (for example, 'I saw a monster and I ran away') and texts told in the third person (for example, 'He saw a monster and he ran away'). The narrator's voice is much less obvious in the second example and this may lead to the impression that the second narrative is more neutral and less open to the workings of the narrator. However, the distinction between third- and first-person narration has questionable value. Booth (1961) refers to it as 'perhaps the most overworked distinction'.

Once it is understood that all texts are narrated, that they all involve the narrative process, the distinction between the first and third person ceases to be a way of identifying the reliable, objective recall of events. Booth qualifies this 'overworked distinction' judgement and adds:

> To say that a story is told in the first or the third person will tell us nothing of importance unless we become more precise and describe how the particular qualities of the narrators relate to specific effects. (page 150)

Rather than focusing on whether the narrator narrates in the first or the third person it is important to see how the narrator relates to the narration. How close is the narrator's relationship to the events narrated? How reliable is the narration? Barthes (1977) suggests that the crucial distinction is not between the first- and third-person narrator but between the 'personal and apersonal' narrators, and that a third-person narrative can be as personal as a first-person narrative, communicating the thoughts and feelings of one particular character.

This can be demonstrated by looking at how easily some third-person narratives can be rewritten in the first person without radically altering the discourse. In the following passage from Jan Mark's *The Snow Maze* Joe has spent playtime being teased by a crowd of children led by Akash. Only Irrum has stood by him:

> Joe did not want to be like Akash, big and strong. He wanted to be like Irrum, small and brave.
>
> At home time Joe ran from school and opened the lonely gate. Then he ran his secret maze.
>
> Akash told the others where he went. They followed Joe, but Joe had his key, and they could not go through the gate into the maze.

The passage is written in the third person but the way in which it is so personally linked to Joe can be seen if it is rewritten merely by changing the first person to the third person:

> I did not want to be like Akash, big and strong. I wanted to be like Irrum, small and brave.
>
> At home time I ran from school and opened the lonely gate. Then I ran my secret maze.
>
> Akash told the others where I went. They followed me, but I had my key, and they could not go through the gate into the maze.

There is as much insight into the personal thought and experience of Joe in the original passage as in the first-person reworking. This explains why it is sometimes difficult to remember whether or not a particular narrative read some time ago was written in the third person.

OVERT AND COVERT

There are varying degrees to which the presence of the narrator can be detected. Chatman speaks of *overt* and *covert* narrators. The narrator who recounts the story in the first person is evidently overt. In Shirley Hughes's *Sea Singing* the overt narrator addresses the narratee in the opening sentence, introducing her story with the question: 'Did I tell you about the time I heard singing coming from the sea?'

However, not all narrators are so obvious. With many narrators there is a degree of covert presence. One way in which the narrator can be detected is when a character's thoughts are reported, the text presenting more than you or I would have seen had we been witnesses to the events of the story. In Jenny Koralek's moving picture book *The Boy and the Cloth of Dreams* (1994) the boy is sent to collect 'threads from the sun and threads from the moon' so that his grandmother can repair the cloth that keeps nightmares away. As he climbs the stairs the text presents thoughts and feelings that would not be visible to a mere observer:

> Gripped with fear, the boy climbed the stairs... and came out on to a flat place on the roof which seemed to be touching the sky... The boy had never before seen anything so beautiful and powerful, so quiet and so certain.
>
> All the same he was terrified.

This narrative is not an objective presentation of events. The narrator is at work. How else would the reader gain an insight into the boy's unspoken thoughts? Booth refers to this as the narrator being:

> ...privileged to know what could not be learned by strictly natural means or limited to realistic vision and inference. Complete privilege is what we usually call omniscience. (page 160)

When the text says the place 'seemed' to be a particular way it begs the question, 'To whom?' The subjective judgements that deem a place beautiful and powerful are insights that are provided by a guiding voice. These are also signs of the narrator becoming more overt. This overt narration is evident in the descriptions of a setting, the judgements that are made about a place, a character or an action. When George's grandmother is described in Dahl's *George's Marvellous Medicine* (1981) as having 'pale brown teeth and a small puckered up mouth' the narrative can be seen as simply providing a verbal imitation of the way she looked. However, this is not a piece of covert narration. Many teachers will recognize the line that actually passes a judgement and expresses the narrator's opinion: 'She had pale brown teeth and a small puckered up mouth like a dog's bottom.' Not the most covert piece of narration!

An understanding of the narrator's presence alerts us to the fact that a narrator may or may not be reliable, a factor that led Booth to classify narrator agents as 'unreliable'. In Martin Waddell's *My Aunty Sal and the Mega-sized Moose* (1996) the stories Sal narrates are often disputed by the narratee, Uncle Jack. The tall stories are presented in a way that causes the reader to question how reliable she is as a narrator.

NARRATIVE LEVEL

Narratives take place at different levels. Returning to Shirley Hughes's *Sea Singing*, the story opens with the overt question from the narrator to the narratee: 'Did I tell you about the time I heard singing coming from the sea?' She goes on to relate the story of the time when she stayed with Morag, an artist who lives in a clifftop house. During this time there was a point at which she heard mysterious singing from the sea. She related this event to Morag. Morag's response was 'I expect it was a selkie.' Morag proceeded to tell the first narrator the story of the selkie who married a fisherman. Morag told how the selkie bride escaped and would only return to visit the children.

At base level, this is a story about a girl who hears the singing. On another level, almost built on to the first story, there is the story of the selkie bride. This is narrated by Morag, who features as a character in the first level of the narrative. Morag's narrative is at a second level. It takes place inside the first narrative.

Therefore, a narrative can consist of a first level within which a second narrative is related. Genette describes the narrator at the first level as *extradiegetic* and labels the narrator who narrates at another level, contained inside the first level, *intradiegetic*. There is the potential for a number of levels to emerge in a narrative, like the layers of a Russian doll.

To apply Genette's terms to Shirley Hughes's story *Sea Singing*, we can say that the girl who is staying beside the sea is an extradiegetic narrator. The whole story is encompassed by her narrative. She operates at the first level of the narration. The story starts with her narrating and finishes with her narrating. Morag, therefore, takes on the role of an intradiegetic narrator. She is narrating a story within the story.

In Jill Murphy's *On the Way Home* (1982) the extradiegetic narrator starts the story with the words: 'Claire had a bad knee, so she set off home to tell her mum all about it.' Claire meets a succession of friends, each of whom asks how she hurt her knee. She answers each of them with a different and elaborate story (including attacks by a big bad wolf, tussles with gorillas and encounters with flying saucers). As Claire relates her story she becomes an intradiegetic narrator operating at another level within the original narrative. After each tall story, the extradiegetic narrator continues to record Claire's progress on the journey home. It is as if the extradiegetic narrator provides a base on which the intradiegetic narrator builds a story.

The narrative within a narrative often bears some significant relation to the first narrative. These internal narratives can have an *explanatory* function. In Ridley's *Krindlekrax* Ruskin discovers that there is a giant crocodile living in the sewers under his street. The question of how the crocodile got there remains unanswered until the night Ruskin's father gets drunk and rambles on about how he lost his job as a zoo keeper. As Ruskin listens, his father unwittingly relates an intradiegetic narrative. He confesses that he was the one who brought the baby crocodile to Lizard Street many years ago.

Genette describes this explanatory function as providing a 'this is why' function, pointing to the function played by this sort of intradiegetic narrative:

> All these narratives answer, explicitly or not, a question of the type 'What events have led to the present situation?' Most often, the curiosity of the intradiegetic listener is only a pretext for replying to the curiosity of the reader... (page 232)

These intradiegetic narratives can also have a *thematic* relationship with the first narratives in which they appear. In the Paul Jennings story *The Busker* (1987) the extradiegetic narrator needs the cash for the taxi that Tania, the girl he wants to take to the cinema, insists he provide if he is to have the privilege of a date with her. As he suffers the dilemma of not having the cash for the taxi he meets a stranger who tells a chilling tale of the busker, a man who tried to buy the love of others. This intradiegetic narrative has no direct link with the boy's dilemma over Tania, but thematically the parallel is clear and teaches the boy a lesson. Tania doesn't get her taxi!

Thirdly, the relating of a narrative can be *an event in itself*. In such cases it is the act of narrating that is important, as when Jenny the dog, in Maurice Sendak's *Higgelty Pigglety Pop! or There Must Be More To Life*, finds what she wants in life. She becomes a performer and acts out a play within the story. Her play is presented as an event within the story but has no real explanatory or thematic link to the extradiegetic narrative. Her acting of the play is an event within the first narrative.

Having made the distinction between narrative level, Genette also distinguishes the narrator who is narrating the story in which he or she is also a participant from the narrator who narrates a story in which he or she plays no part. Genette terms the narrator who is present in the story being narrated a *homodiegetic* narrator. The narrator who is absent from the story he or she narrates is called a *heterodiegetic* narrator. He points out that the narrator can be the story's 'star' or 'a mere bystander'.

Both types of narrator are used in children's literature. The homodiegetic voice of Tom in the 'Tom and Pippo' stories by Helen Oxenbury is a popular example, recounting his life with Pippo. There is an interesting example of a heterodiegetic narrator in Shirley Hughes's *Sea Singing*. As we have seen earlier, Morag tells the girl the story of the selkie bride. She does not appear in the story and says she learned it from her grandmother. It appears that she is a heterodiegetic narrator narrating a story in which she plays no part. However, there is a subtle link. In the selkie story the bride would reappear and leave gifts such as coral beads and mother-of-pearl boxes. As Morag is pictured finishing the story, the illustration shows that she is sitting beside some objects, which are the same as those previously depicted as the presents. It is a subtle and suggestive link that plays with the idea of the narrator's relation to the narrative.

IN PRACTICE: AUTHORS AND NARRATORS

The practical implications of the theory outlined in the first part of this chapter result in some basic learning objectives and activities. However, it should by now be clear that the narrative process is a complex part of the theoretical basis for this book. The primary practical consideration is that an understanding of the process of narration can enhance the teacher's own critical awareness of how texts communicate. How that process is accomplished varies greatly from story to story. The first practical implication is that an awareness that a narrative process is at work in stories can make a difference to how we understand and work with the texts we read in class. Reflecting on the narrative process in the stories we use can alter the way in which we read them.

In Jennings' *The Busker* the extradiegetic narrator starts the story with a row at home. Then he meets the mysterious storyteller on the beach. The attitudes adopted and mannerisms used when reading the words of the two different narrators can vary. I have made use of my awareness of who is doing the narrating at given points in a story, whose voice is telling, what they know, what they have yet to discover and how reliable those listening to the story will consider them to be. This aspect of poetics is worth working on because children's stories often use a complex mix of narrative strategies. I have come across the 'Tom and Pippo' stories used in nursery settings, yet *Tom and Pippo and the Washing Machine* (1988) provides a fine example of the unreliability of a narrator. At the close of the story, Tom narrates:

> The trouble is, I know Pippo's going to get dirty again. I can't stop him playing in muddy places.

With appropriate discussion, young children can often pick out in the accompanying illustration the fact that Tom is the one dropping stones in the muddy puddle, splashing the water over Pippo. They also spring to Pippo's defence, pointing out that he doesn't looks happy about the situation in which he finds himself. In many ways the story is a simple one, yet it contains this complex disparity between what the overt narrator tells us and what the reader interprets.

Such stories should provide an opportunity to explore the various levels and the differing relationship between the narrator and the narrative. There is also a need to keep the narrative process clear so that the switching of levels does not frustrate children who are baffled by the complexity. As the narration switches from one narrator to another they need to know who is doing the narrating.

Bearing in mind the complexity of this process, it is crucial to also remember that the learning objectives throughout this book are designed for the whole primary age range, to be modified by the individual teacher working with a particular age group. Having said this, the following objectives are suggested as practical responses to the above sections of theory. Children should be taught to:

✧ develop an awareness of the various participants at work in the narrative process and be introduced to some of the issues that surround the role of the narrator;

✧ critically appraise the narrator of a story, questioning the narrator's relationship to the story and his or her reliability;

✧ understand the way in which a narrative can operate at various levels, looking at the way in which stories within stories function.

As with all the specific literary terms, the teacher must make the judgement as to whether or not to use the label applied to a part of the literary process. I find children, from a very young age, like using 'big words' but it is the underlying ideas that can enrich the reading of texts, not the glossary.

The following suggestions can be used to help to translate the theory into activities.

WORK WITH THE TERM 'NARRATOR'

Children can be given an insight into the different roles in the process of communicating a narrative. The role of narrator can be explored, primarily by using the term to describe the voice that addresses the children from within the text. This will not be at odds with the aim that children should identify the role of the author. If anything, it will strengthen that aim.

Children can build up a picture of the narrator in a text. The points at which the narrator is overt can be pointed out. There may even be scope for building up a collection of these signs of overt narration to collate a picture of the narrator. For example, in *Alfie Gives a Hand* (1983) the class could collect a set of notes that describes what can be gathered about the narrator from the text. One way of pointing out the presence of the narrator is to ask, 'If we had been there what would we have seen?' Had we been at the party in the Alfie story would we have *seen* Alfie's thought that 'he might leave his blanket at home'? The line between overt and covert narration is subject to subtleties but there are obvious instances of overt narration such as overt 'I...' statements in the narration.

The homodiegetic narrator narrates the story in which he or she is a participant and, as a result, there is often a wealth of 'I...' statements that can build up a picture of that narrator. In other narratives it is a matter of locating the overt points in the narrative, as when the narrator of Jones's *Nicobobinus* narrates one of Nicobobinus's narrow scrapes, then slips in the comment: 'But I think he was lucky in one respect...'

QUESTION THE NARRATOR

At any point in the story, the readers can come up with questions or disagreements they could put to the narrator of the text. Having read the opening of a story, ask the children to list questions they would put to the narrator. These may question the narrator's account of events or the opinions they express. One way of focusing the class's mind on who is being questioned is for the teacher to read a part (or parts) of the text. It needs to be made clear that the teacher's voice is the voice of the narrator. When the reading stops, questions can be directed to the teacher who has assumed this role. The teacher need not and possibly cannot answer them. Some questions will be answered by the narrative as it continues. Some questions are meant to be left open.

After reading the opening of Paul Jennings' *The Gizmo* (in which the narrator confesses to stealing the Gizmo) to a class, the following questions to the narrator were listed:

- ✧ Why did you steal the Gizmo?
- ✧ Weren't you scared of the shopkeeper?
- ✧ Would you ever steal another thing?
- ✧ Do you think you should have stolen from the man?
- ✧ Wasn't it wrong?
- ✧ What if he (the shopkeeper) finds out?

A list of questions like this doesn't just make enquiries; it can also raise issues of disagreement. When the narrator ends up being tortured by the Gizmo he stole, the narration can lead a class to take issue with the narrator. There are those who feel he is getting his just desserts and those who point to the fact that, by his own admission, he had never stolen anything before and he did try to return the booty.

The disagreement can be structured into a worksheet format. Using two columns you can make a list, in the left-hand column, of overt comments or opinions expressed by the narrator. The children can then record alongside these, in the right-hand column, their responses. Activities such as these can draw out the extent to which the narrator can be relied upon and the bias of the narrator.

PRIVILEGE

As we saw earlier, Booth described the narrator's inside view into the inner life of another character as a kind of privilege. The narrator can present the unspoken thoughts of a character, as when the narrator of *Alfie Gives a Hand* presents Alfie's thought that he might leave his blanket at home next time he goes to a party.

Children can take on this privileged role, presenting their own narration of the unspoken thoughts of a character in a story. These can be written in 'thought bubbles', drawing on the use of the method of presenting thoughts in comics such as *The Beano*. Children can draw similar bubbles stemming from a character at a particular point in the story and write the thoughts they think a character could be having. For example, what is Max thinking during his 'wild rumpus' with the wild things? By assuming this privileged position, the children are being asked to span the gap between what is known by the straightforward witness of events and the privileged knowledge often displayed by a narrator.

A RANGE OF NARRATORS

The classification devised by Genette can be used by a teacher in seeking to introduce children to the full range of types of narrator. Within the literature available for use in class there will be a variety of extra- and intradiegetic narrators, hetero- and homodiegetic narrators. As stated previously, the terms themselves may or may not be mentioned but the teacher can use the distinctions as a means of choosing texts to read in class that adopt varying narrative styles. The distinctions can also be pointed out, possibly in simplified terms, to the class.

THE FUNCTION OF THE INTRADIEGETIC NARRATIVE

When a story within a story arises it is worth asking what function it performs. It was noted earlier that there are three potential functions: the narrative can be explanatory, thematic or an event in itself. Children can be shown the job the narrative is doing within the whole story. It can sometimes be worth imagining what the rest of the story would be like if that intradiegetic narrative was not there. Highlighting the role of such narratives can lead children to use them in their own story writing. The rule of thumb here is, on encountering such narratives, to look at the purpose they are serving.

STORIES INSIDE STORIES

Children can produce their own intradiegetic narratives. Such an activity can be used as a speaking task for younger children as they develop their own creative storytelling, or as a writing task for older children.

A focus needs to be found inside a narrative. For example, looking at *Alfie Gives a Hand*, Alfie is very attached to his blanket. An intradiegetic narrative could be devised in which, on the way to the party, Alfie or Alfie's mum recounts where the blanket came from or why Alfie became so attached to it. There is the potential for a story about the trauma that arose when he once lost the blanket. Either the teacher can identify a point in a narrative where there is this potential or older children may be able to locate their own examples.

The activity will be enriched by you providing some other examples of stories within stories. These can be very brief, as when the frog prince recounts the story of how he was turned into a frog. It is also useful to outline the main functions of intradiegetic narratives (listed above as explanatory, thematic and stories that are events in themselves). It is worth noting good examples of these stories within stories while reading children's literature and gauging the function they serve.

A NARRATIVE OF NARRATIVES

Children can produce their own compilation of narratives on a particular theme. This can often involve the process of interviewing other people. For a collection of narratives on the theme of being lost, for example, children can interview parents, younger siblings and grandparents, asking them to tell stories about their experiences of being lost. The children can then record the narratives they were told. On another level, there is also an interesting narrative to be found in the record of how they found these stories.

The resultant collection will involve some extradiegetic narration about their research along the lines of:

> I wanted to find out about journeys. I asked my grandparents to tell me about the longest journey they had ever made.

This will lead to the intradiegetic narration, such as:

> My grandmother told me about her journey from Somalia to France...

The stories can be very brief, as when younger children build up their compilation as a group effort:

> We decided to make a book about parties. We asked lots of people to tell us about the best party they had ever been to.
>
> Rochelle went to ask her gran. She lives a long way away. Rochelle took a cassette recorder. Her mum made Gran a cup of tea, then she told the story about a party they had on VE day.

Rochelle's story will eventually give way to another child's. There is the story of her Gran and the VE day party but there is also the story of Rochelle's search for the story. This sort of activity involves children in taking on the role of the narrator and experiencing the various levels at which narratives can be written.

POINT OF VIEW

Whatever happens in the news today one thing is certain, the account of events will not be a straightforward matter in which all sides agree on one narrative. It is not uncommon to find the same situation – a strike, for example – being recorded in completely different ways. The union leader will give one account of a strike; the management will give a different account. The same events, the same situation can generate completely different stories. This is because a story is related in an act of communication. When talks break down in a dispute the two different sides will recount the story of what happened from their viewpoint. Unless they were actually in the room when talks broke down, the hearer relies on the reports of those who were. Such reports are never simple. Narratives are always presented from a particular viewpoint.

Throughout a story, too, the events are being recounted from a particular *point of view*. This will be the viewpoint that influences the way in which the material in a narrative is related.

Adele Berlin gives a helpful illustration of the way in which point of view works. She asks us to imagine seeing the same play at the theatre and in a televised version. At the theatre the spectator sits and has one point of view. Various pieces of stagecraft direct the attention to a particular focus, such as when the big speech comes and the speaker takes centre stage. Filmed versions are different. The story is filtered through the perspective of the camera's eye. The camera directs our attention to the speaker of the big speech by giving a close up of his or her face. Its lens directs our perspective on the events. It defines and alters our point of view. This might explain the other term used to describe 'point of view'; some theorists use the term *focalisation*.

The narrating of a story is done in a way that presents the events from a point of view. This point of view can alter during the narrative. Chatman takes the phrase 'point of view' and suggests three ways in which the term is commonly used that can be applied to the narrating of a story.

✧ Point of view can be a matter of *perception*. Events can be literally recounted through someone's eyes, restricted to their perception of events. (For example, 'She looked round and saw a goblin.')

✧ Point of view can be a matter of *conception*. Events can be viewed from the conceptual point of view, relating things to someone's opinions, ideas, expectations and so on. This will be an internal relating to a conceptual point of view. (For example, 'From her point of view the goblin's offer was wonderful.')

✧ Point of view can be a matter of *interest*. The things that happen may work for or against an individual and, as a result, may be different from their point of view. Chelsea winning the FA Cup is great from the point of view of a Chelsea supporter but not so pleasing from the point of view of someone who supports the losing side. It's a matter of interests being served or not served that makes something beneficial from a particular point of view. So when the goblin in *Rumpelstiltskin* helps the girl, 'from her point of view it was to prove a mixed blessing'.

A narrative is often presented in relation to a variety of points of view. In Dahl's *James and the Giant Peach*, as James enters the peach the action is related from his point of view. As he entered the peach stone his:

> ...large frightened eyes travelled slowly round the room.
>
> The creatures... were all watching him intently.
>
> Creatures?
>
> Or were they insects?

The 'creatures' know what they are; the narrator knows what they are; as the story develops both James and the reader discover what they are. However, at this stage in the story the focus of the perception and conception is James. The narrative is relating the story to what *James* sees and how he sees it; hence the 'frightened eyes' and the use of the term 'creatures'. This is James's point of view.

Later in the story, James and the creatures are inside the giant peach as it is released from the tree and rolls away, an event that is initially described in Chapter 15 of the book from the point of view of James's two evil aunts who are in the garden searching for him. As they hunt for James the text relates Aunt Spiker saying: 'What's that awful noise?' The point of view is hers. She has heard a noise. The narrative continues:

> Both women swung round to look.
>
> The noise, of course, had been caused by the giant peach crashing through the fence that surrounded it, and now, gathering speed every second, it came rolling across the garden towards the place where Aunt Sponge and Aunt Spiker were standing.
>
> They gaped. They screamed. They started to run. They panicked. They both got in each other's way... each one of them was thinking only about saving herself.

The two aunts turn to look. At this point the narrative briefly relates an event (the crash that caused the noise) from an external point of view. Then we return to the point of view of the two aunts as the narrative relates them perceiving the peach coming towards them. Their internal feelings are given as they panic and think of saving themselves. Finally, 'the mighty peach was upon them. There was a crunch'.

Later in the story, the same events are related from the point of view of James and the creatures inside the peach, a 'terrible journey' in which the end of the two Aunts is related from a different point of view:

> And when it went *BUMP!*, and the Centipede had shouted, '*That* was Aunt Sponge!' and then *BUMP!* again, and '*That* was Aunt Spiker!' there had been a tremendous burst of cheering all round.

The flattening of the two villains involves a couple of bumps because events are related from the point of view of those inside the peach.

The section from *James and the Giant Peach*, quoted on page 109, in which the aunts are in the garden, can also illustrate two different ways of categorising the point of view from which the story is being related. Bal (1985) distinguishes between character-bound focalisation and external focalisation (the term 'focalisation' being used instead of 'point of view'). Point of view can be bound to a character or it can describe an external perception of events. In the example of the two aunts in the garden the character-bound perception ('Both women swung round to look') is momentarily interrupted by an external replay of the events that caused the noise (the peach crashing through the fence). After that, the point of view is, once again, bound up with the two aunts. The point of view has switched from them hearing and looking to refer to what you or I would have seen as observers of the events. It then switches back to their viewpoint. The relating of events can be bound to a particular character's point of view or related from an external position. It is worth noting that the point of view will not always be that of the narrator. The narrator may, in the course of a narrative, relate events from several points of view, as happens in the examples quoted above.

Bal also draws a distinction between the perceptible and the non-perceptible. The object of a character's point of view may be perceptible, as when James sees the creatures inside the peach. Anybody else in that room would have seen what James saw. The object of his point of view was perceptible. The non-perceptible are the things another person would not see. Bal cites the examples of a character's dream being presented or his or her unspoken thoughts. When Jack, in Paul Jennings' *The Gizmo Again* (1995) looks around a corner to see who is coming – 'Then I see who it is... It is not my mum. It is the last person in the world that I want it to be. It is Micky O'Shea' – the point of view switches from the non-perceptible (the observer could not see the thoughts about who he wants it to be) to the perceptible (the observer could see Micky O'Shea).

INDICATING POINT OF VIEW

The point of view in a narrative can shift, as was evident in the section from *James and the Giant Peach*. Certain indicators in a narrative will guide the reader's awareness of these shifts in point of view. The indicators adopt a varying degree of subtlety. Three of the most common ways of indicating point of view are the verbs used, the names applied to characters and the use of description.

VERBS

The use of the word 'saw' and other verbs that describe perception act as blatant indicators of the act of viewing things. In Rose Impey's telling of *Rumpelstiltskin* (1992) the little man jumps in through the window to the room where the young girl is expected to weave straw into gold. The previous night he carried out the task for her and now:

> ...up she jumps and lets in that little wee man. He stands there grinning. *He* can see what *she's* thinking...

In this case the point of view shifts to the little man. He 'sees' the non-perceptible, 'what *she's* thinking', an indication of the way he sees the situation from his point of view. Although the word 'saw' is a particularly powerful indicator of point of view, other verbal indicators can focus the action in a similar way. When Michael Rosen (1983) describes his experience of hearing his son under the table – 'Better have a look. Oh no. He's got a dead mouse in his hand' – the point of view is Rosen's, not his son's.

This device isn't limited to the act of seeing. In Tony Ross's *I'm Coming to Get You* (1984) Tommy Brown 'thought he heard a bump outside the window'. In a narrative, any verbal indicators that locate the perceptions or the thoughts act as an indicator of the point of view.

NAMES

The use of naming to develop a point of view is often subtle and persuasive. The narrative names characters or items in a particular way that can denote the point of view to which the narrative is being related and fill out some of the non-perceptible thoughts and feelings that guide it. For example, in Dick King Smith's *The Sheep-Pig* (1983) the names applied to Babe, the pig, depend on the point of view from which the narrative is related. Farmer Hogget calls him 'Pig' throughout. The other animals, and Babe himself, know him by his name 'Babe'. This can be seen in the switch between points of view in the following extract from the book:

> The very next morning Farmer Hogget decided that he would see if the pig would like to come, when he went round the sheep with Fly. I'm daft, he thought, grinning to himself. He did not tell his wife.
>
> Seeing him walk down the yard, crook in hand, and

> hearing him call Fly, Babe was about to settle down for an after-breakfast nap when to his surprise he heard the farmer's voice again.
>
> 'Come, Pig,' said Farmer Hogget...

The first paragraph is told from Farmer Hogget's point of view, so Babe is referred to as 'the pig', whereas in the next paragraph the pig is the one 'seeing' the action. Accordingly, in this paragraph, the pig is given his name 'Babe'. The naming denotes more than just a title. There is something in the use of different names that can indicate who is using the name and what the usage tells us about their point of view. Later, in the field, Hogget tries some sheep-dog instructions on the pig:

> 'Away to me, Pig!' he said softly.
>
> Without a moment's hesitation Babe began the long outrun to the right.
>
> Quite what Farmer Hogget had expected to happen, he could never afterwards clearly remember. What he had not expected was that the pig would run round to the rear of the flock...

Later, as Hogget discovers the pig's unique abilities, Babe is named 'the sheep-pig'. The relationship develops until, at the very end of the story when Babe triumphs, the naming is changed once again:

> 'That'll do,' said Farmer Hogget to his sheep-pig. 'That'll do.'

Babe has become *his* sheep-pig, indicating a conceptual point of view that has evolved through the course of the narrative.

DESCRIPTION

The description of a particular scene or action can be narrated in a way that focuses the event through a particular character's point of view. When Babe in *The Sheep-Pig* is suspected of attacking the sheep, Farmer Hogget is about to shoot him. This event is described from Babe's point of view:

> He saw the boss... carrying something in the crook of one arm, a long thing, a kind of black shiny tube... the boss was pointing the black shiny tube at him, and he sat down again and waited, supposing that perhaps it was some machine for giving out food...

The reader will realise this is a gun but the narrative point of view is Babe's and he has no idea it could be such a thing.

A narrative is mediated and part of this process of mediation will involve relating the narrative to various points of view. These focalise the narrative, tying the relating of events to a particular perspective.

IN PRACTICE: POINT OF VIEW

An understanding of point of view focuses attention on the perspective from which a narrative is related. In looking at this area of literary theory, the sort of learning objectives covered should include the aims that children learn to:

- identify the presence of various points of view in a narrative;
- look at the events in a story in relation to the point of view of a particular character;
- reflect on the thoughts and feelings that will motivate various participants in a narrative.

The following activities give some insights into ways in which these objectives can be translated into practice.

QUESTIONS IN READING

This area of theory furnishes the teacher with a way of questioning children about the stories they read or have read to them. A narrative can be read and discussed from the points of view of various characters . This was shown to be quite pointed in the extracts from Dick King-Smith's *The Sheep-Pig*. A picture book such as David McKee's *Not Now, Bernard* can also make interesting material for this sort of discussion. The perception throughout the narrative is that of an observer of events. It is not fixed to one character. However, Bernard warns his parents of the monster who eventually eats him but they continually dismiss him with the words, 'Not now, Bernard.' The interesting contrast is between what Bernard saw and thought and what either of his parents saw and thought. The monster in the garden is treated quite differently from Bernard's point of view and that of his mum.

While reading a story, questions about what a character sees, feels, wants and thinks can reinforce the concept of point of view. This can involve stopping the reading of a story and asking children how things are going from a particular character's viewpoint, how a particular character feels and what he or she wants. Such questioning can be enhanced by the teacher's recognition that certain passages lend themselves to the consideration of a particular character's point of view.

THOUGHT BUBBLES

Children are often asked to draw a scene from a story. An addition to such a drawing can be made by cutting out 'thought bubble' shapes. These can be pasted on to a picture to display the thoughts harboured by a particular character. The drama activities noted later in this section can help in developing an idea of what these thoughts could be. This can be a particularly provocative group task. Stopping a story in the middle of an event, the teacher can ask groups of children quickly to draw the event. They then discuss and complete 'thought bubbles' for the various characters. It can result in discussion as to what a particular character knows and believes. Recently, working with a class on *The Tempest*, this provoked an interesting question from Lotoya (aged 8). Prompted by the group's disagreement over whether Prospero was intending to be good or bad, she asked, 'Do the bad people think they're doing bad things?' And the debate started...

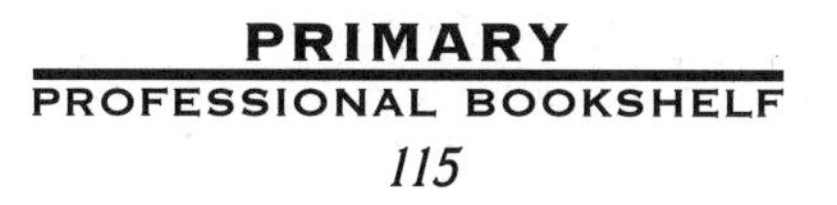

RECORDING THE NARRATIVE FROM A POINT OF VIEW

The two activities outlined below relate to this one idea, namely that when examining and recording the events in a story, children can attempt to look at them from the point of view of a particular character.

DIARIES

Diaries can limit the attention to one point of view. Having read Hughes's *Alfie Gives a Hand*, children can record the events in the story in diary form, taking separate pages for the day before the party and the day of the party. The diary could be one written by Alfie or by Alfie's mum.

A more extended narrative, such as *The Tempest*, can be recorded in more stages, but here again the diary can be that of a particular character, reflecting the amount the character knows, the opinions he or she has and the events as they are experienced.

FRAMES

Frames can help children to focus on presenting a particular character's point of view. The child draws a simple square in which he or she presents a character's perspective at a given point in the story. This can be an interesting way of visualising how an event appears to a particular individual. Sometimes the frame can be filled with a picture showing what the character can see. Or it can be filled with writing that records the child's conceptual point of view. The example shown on page 117 is drawn from work on *The Tempest* and presents Ferdinand's point of view as he slaves for Prospero.

Focusing on what a particular character can or cannot see can provide some interesting interaction with a story. In one of the traditional tales about the German joker Till Owlyglass, in Rosen's *The Wicked Tricks of Till Owlyglass* (1990), Till wants to show his father that he is an innocent child and that people complain about him without provocation. To do this he rides through the town on a horse, sitting immediately in front of his

Prospero doesn't like me.
He's making me a slave.
He has magic powers
so I can't fight him.
He won't let me see Miranda.

father. Sure enough, people complain about his rudeness and Till points out that his father has been there all along, with himself innocently sitting in front of him. This is to be his father's point of view. But what the passers-by saw was Till sticking his tongue out at them. They had a different point of view.

Frames can be produced for different parts of the story, resulting in a set of frames that show how, for example, Ferdinand comes to have a different view of Prospero as *The Tempest* progresses.

CONNECTIONS

The ways in which a set of characters view each other can be explored by looking at the connections between them. A simple chart can demonstrate these interactions. This is an activity that can work well with Key Stage 1 children, focusing on the thoughts and feelings of particular characters. (The younger the children are, the more they may need help with the actual drawing of the chart). Taking four characters from a story, their names can be written in the corners of a sheet of paper. The children draw arrows from one person to another, leaving a space in the middle of the arrow. The space is then filled by the response of the character in the corner where the arrow begins to the character in the other corner, as shown. The connections can be built up until every character is allocated arrows showing their viewpoint on others in the story.

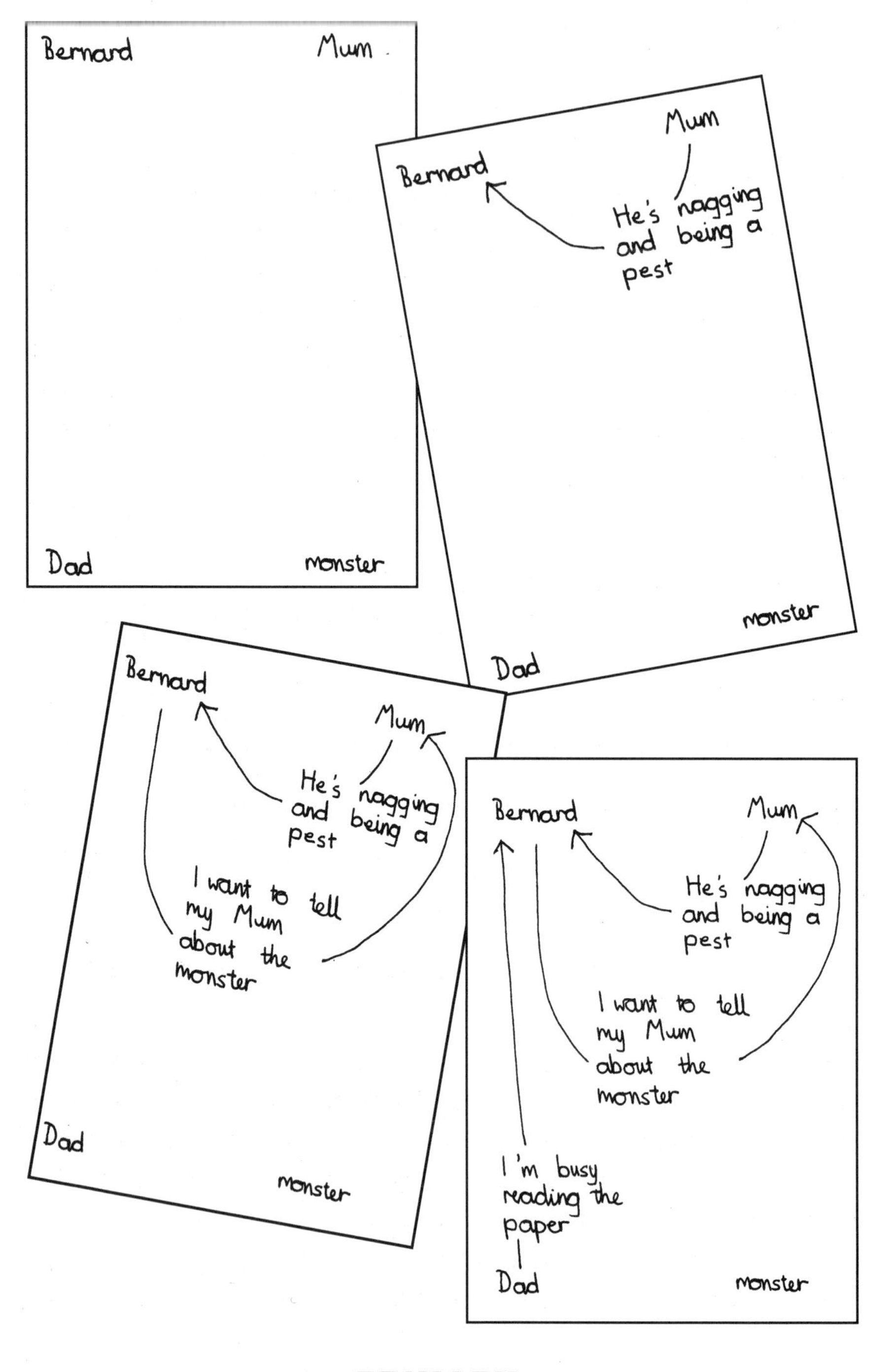

A variation on this idea is to include 'me' as one of the corners. The main purpose of this corner is to provide a way of inputting the child's point of view as a reader interacting with the various characters on the chart.

SNAKES AND LADDERS

The ways in which events in a story work for or against the interest of a character can be identified and explored using the symbols of a snake and a ladder. The activity requires a list of events from a story that involves a particular character. This could be produced by the teacher, a child or a group of children working together. The collection of events can be marked with a 'ladder' if they work in the character's interest. Or they can be marked with a 'snake' if they work against the character's interest.

Joe finds the Secret maze

Akash makes fun of Joe

The symbols act as a convenient way of exploring the 'interest' aspect of point of view.

DRAMA AS A WAY OF EXPLORING POINT OF VIEW

Drama can provide a medium through which children can participate in the point of view of a particular character. Here again, the activity can take the reader beyond the point of view inscribed in the text. It involves the exercise of the treatment of characters as open constructs, an issue discussed in Chapter 2.

Hendy (1994) presents a variety of drama activities with the suggestion that they can be used in relation to stories. Through the following activities, drawn from Hendy's article, children can focus on the events in a story relating them to a particular point of view. Hendy's article covers a broader use of drama and has many useful ideas. Four that can be particularly effective at teasing out point of view in a story include:

SCENE INVENTING

A group can act out a scene that is not in a story, presenting invented dialogue and actions (for example, Goldilocks speaking to the Three Bears). In this way the same characters are brought into a new scenario.

COLLECTIVE ROLE-PLAY

A group can role-play a single character. The teacher and other children then question the group who are acting the role of the character. The group reflect together and produce collectively agreed answers.

HOT SEATING

One child in the group is placed on the 'hot seat' and takes on the role of a character in the story. The child then faces questions from the rest of the group, answering them from the point of view of that particular character.

THOUGHT TRACKING

A group can devise a 'still image' in which participants pose to represent a particular scene from the story. Having presented this still-life scene, the participants say how they think the character they are acting felt and what he or she thought at that point in time.

GET INSIDE THE STORY

Marsh (1996) shows how the sort of activities suggested above can be practically applied to a picture book such as Sendak's *Where the Wild Things Are*. Among the reasons she gives for the practical uses of drama in the exploration of a picture book she states:

> Basing drama activities on a book can enable the children to get inside the story and enhance their understanding and appreciation of it... Children can become, or interact with, the characters in the story and begin to empathise with them and understand their motives a little more. (page 13)

CRITICAL AWARENESS OF NARRATIVE

This chapter has looked at some of the factors at work in the ways of telling a story. The complexities of the narrative process and the effect of point of view should illustrate the distinction made at the start of this chapter between the story and its narration. Stories are not a simple mimicking of events such as you or I would have seen had we been present. They involve a process of narrating.

It is because it is such a pervasive part of story that an understanding of the narrative process can be so useful in the classroom. Such an understanding provides the means of demonstrating the various ways in which the narrative act takes place in the stories we read. We can respond to that narrative act with interest, suspicion, agreement or questioning. In an environment in which children are so open to the influence of the media and the many ways of telling, the critical awareness of narrative prompts a realisation that someone is narrating any story. This is a valuable piece of awareness.

CHAPTER 5

THE RANGE OF STORIES

My mum read 'Sunny Stories' at school. They are her one abiding memory of infant education. At various points in the day the teacher would collect the class together and pull out a *Sunny Story*. They came in yellow covers, and if it was a battered cover it was a good story and if it was pristine it was not so good. If the teacher ever read a different type of story it either didn't make much impact or my mum wasn't paying much attention!

What is noticeable today is the range of stories that have been brought into the contemporary primary curriculum. If I look through the planning folders for the teachers I work with I see a vast range of stories, including fables, modern novels, classics, picture books and Greek myths. A combination of the range of books publishers now make available and the curriculum innovations that have brought these into the classroom has left us with a primary curriculum in which there is a vast range of stories to work with.

Thus far we have looked at individual stories examining the different workings that make up the poetics of the texts. Much of this has looked at elements that are common to texts, such as the linking of events or the activity of a narrator. In this chapter the perspective broadens to look at the range of stories teachers work with. It is not my aim to take an in-depth look at the task of co-ordinating the school's use of its book stock or practical issues such as how books are stored, where and when they are read and so on. Rather this chapter focuses on the principle that there is a wide range of stories available to teachers. The job of the teacher therefore involves introducing children to this range and making them aware of their varied reactions to the diverse types of story available to them.

In the drafts of the National Curriculum there have been various attempts to indicate just what it is children are supposed to read. The Cox Report (DES, 1989) went so far as to list a page of authors whose work met the criteria by which they judged literature suitable for the primary school. This was greeted with complaints from several of the writers whose names were featured on the approved list! Subsequently, the emphasis has been on recommending the types of literature that should be used (this emphasis can also be seen in the guidelines for the National Literacy Project).

At Key Stage 1 the National Curriculum programme of study for English recommends the reading of:

✧ poems and stories with familiar settings and those based on imaginary or fantasy worlds;
✧ books and poems written by significant children's authors;
✧ retellings of traditional folk and fairy stories;
✧ stories and poems from a range of cultures;
✧ stories, poems and chants containing patterned and predictable language;
✧ stories and poems that are particularly challenging in terms of length or vocabulary.

At Key Stage 2 the programme of study recommends the reading of:

✧ a range of modern fiction by significant children's authors;
✧ some long-established children's fiction;
✧ a range of good quality modern poetry;
✧ some classic poetry;
✧ texts drawn from a variety of cultures and traditions;
✧ myths, legends and traditional stories.

In Scotland, the guidelines for the teaching of English 5–14 state that at Level E children should be able to *'Identify some similarities and differences of form and content in examples of texts from a variety of genres, and comment on how these reflect the text's purposes'*.

This chapter is divided into two sections. The first looks at some theoretical aspects of the range of literature, including the various genres children read and how we can involve them in reflection on the concept of genre. The second section looks at the range of texts used in the primary context and ways of working within that range.

GENRE

The term *genre* is derived from the Latin 'genus', a term many of us came across in biology lessons that described a way of grouping biologically diverse plants and creatures. Similarly, there are groups of texts that are of a particular genus. In many bookshops, books belonging to a specified genre will have a section of their own, so 'crime' books, for example, will be placed in a separate section from 'science fiction'. In these ways various stories are grouped under headings that indicate a familial connection.

HOW GENRES ARE CLASSIFIED

The classification of a group of books as a genre is a complex issue. At what point do a few similarities between different works become a genre? Why do we speak of 'science fiction' as a genre but not 'stories that contain plumbers'? Todorov (1990) raises the issue in this way:

> It is always possible to discover a property common to two texts, and thus to put them together in a class. Is there any virtue in calling the result of such a combination a 'genre'? (page 17)

Some sort of convention must be conceived if a set of texts are to be classed as a genre, otherwise there is nothing to stop the grouping of a few books bearing a slight resemblance into a whole new category. Grandparents feature in Roald Dahl's *George's Marvellous Medicine*, Dyan Sheldon and Gary Blythe's *The Whales' Song* and numerous other stories but that hardly merits the new genre of 'grandparent fiction'.

Todorov identifies the *historical* dimension to the origin of genres, suggesting we use the term genre to apply to classes of texts that, in the course of time, have historically been grouped together in a particular class. An example of such a historical gathering of diverse tales can be seen in the genre of the fairy tale.

However, Todorov also suggests that history alone does not provide an adequate reason for classifying texts in a particular genre. It may be possible to identify that, historically, two texts have been classed under the heading 'comedy'. But this historical classification is not the only way of giving credence to the recognition that they belong to a particular genre. Readers themselves can also identify *similarities* between the texts that validate this classification. Todorov points out that it is possible to look within historically classified genres and see why a certain set of texts were classed together in a particular way. So, for example, P.D. James's novels will be classified with those of Colin Dexter in a section labelled 'crime'. Historically, this has been the case – but without the verdict of history it is still possible to see the similarities between such stories. The recognition of a resemblance between texts causes them to be classed in a genre. Genres are then handed down through communities of readers. They become institutionalised. In the end the perception of similarities between texts must go hand in hand with the historical recognition of those texts as sharing some commonality.

WHY GENRES MATTER

For readers the main effects genre will entail will be upon:
- the way they influence a reader's selection of texts;
- the expectations they engender;
- the way in which the reader classifies texts as part of an ongoing reading experience.

GENRE AND SELECTION

Genre can influence the reader's selection of reading material. As a teenager my first question in a bookshop was always 'Where are the mystery stories?' Genre was helping me as a reader to locate the sort of text I wanted to read. Over time, genre will help young readers to select the sort of books they want to read. In my experience, as children first start to read novels they often develop a liking for a particular author or type of story to the exclusion of others. The job of the teacher is to broaden that liking to include other texts within that genre.

GENRE AND EXPECTATION

As we approach a text, there will be all sorts of expectations that will affect our reading. Dubrow (1988) presents an interesting example of the way in which readers' grasp of genre influences their expectations on approaching the reading of a text. Her study of genre opens with the following passage which she asks us to assume is from a novel called *Murder at Marplethorpe*. It opens with the words:

> The clock on the mantlepiece said ten thirty, but someone had suggested recently that the clock was wrong. As the figure of the dead woman lay on the bed in the front room, a no less silent figure glided rapidly from the house. The only sounds to be heard were the ticking of that clock and the loud wailing of an infant. (page 1)

She then asks her readers to re-read the passage, this time reading it as if it were from a 'formation novel' – the sort of life story that traces the growing-up of a hero (Dickensian examples include *David Copperfield*). Dubrow calls this imaginary novel *The Personal History of David Marplethorpe*. It is worth trying this, re-reading the section, noting the features of the scene again and thinking of their significance. What would be the significance of the mistimed clock and the silent figure?

When read as an example from the first genre, our expectations are centred on the clue of the clock telling the wrong time. We assume the dead woman to be the victim. The silent figure must be a murderer. When read as an example of the second genre, the clock may appear symbolic. The dead woman is tragically placed at the start of young David

Marplethorpe's life, he probably being the crying child. The silent figure may be sending for medical help. In both cases the different expectations are prompted by the readers' usual expectations when reading texts in a particular genre. In Todorov's words, genres function as 'horizons of expectation' (page 18). They indicate to readers what type of text they are about to read and, in doing so, suggest how to read it.

GENRE AND CLASSIFICATION

The use of genre as a means of classifying texts underlies this creation of a 'horizon of expectation'. Stories fit into a particular genre. They also increase the reader's experience of that particular genre. Genres are not identifiable by terms set in tablets of stone. The shifting nature of genres can undermine attempts at classification (which may explain why we have come so far in this chapter without listing a set of genres). In many video shops the 'action' film now seems an established genre separated from that of the 'thriller'. The question that underpins the use of genre as a means of classification is how are the texts to be classified? In his article on the classification of stories Warlow (1977) makes the point that:

> ...all serious discussion of children's reading has been hopelessly confused by the lack of mutually exclusive categories. Conventional phrases such as 'adventure story' (most stories surely consist of some sort of adventure), 'fantasy' (any fiction is in some sense a fantasy), 'animal story' (what have *Aesop's Fables*, *Black Beauty*, *Tarka the Otter* and *Rupert Bear* in common save the number of their characters' legs?) offer no basis for analysis. (page 99)

Warlow works from the question children will often ask about a story that they read, 'Is it true?' and presents a chart for classifying texts 'according to their similarity or dissimilarity to the external world as we see it and generally understand it' (page 99).

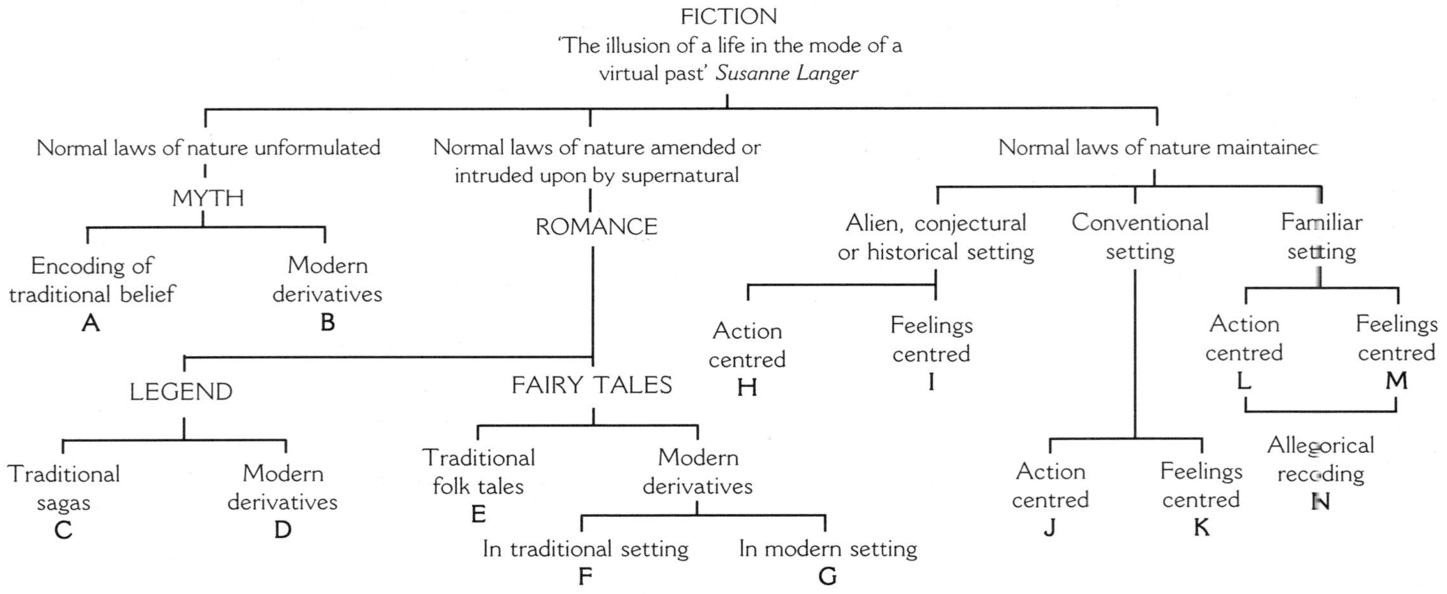

FICTION
'The illusion of a life in the mode of a virtual past' *Susanne Langer*

- Normal laws of nature unformulated
  - MYTH
    - Encoding of traditional belief **A**
    - Modern derivatives **B**
- Normal laws of nature amended or intruded upon by supernatural
  - ROMANCE
    - LEGEND
      - Traditional sagas **C**
      - Modern derivatives **D**
    - FAIRY TALES
      - Traditional folk tales **E**
      - Modern derivatives
        - In traditional setting **F**
        - In modern setting **G**
- Normal laws of nature maintained
  - Alien, conjectural or historical setting
    - Action centred **H**
    - Feelings centred **I**
  - Conventional setting
    - Action centred **J**
    - Feelings centred **K**
  - Familiar setting
    - Action centred **L**
    - Feelings centred **M**
    - Allegorical recording **N**

EXAMPLES

A	**B**	**C**	**D**	**E**	**F**	**G**
Greek	Kingsley	Homer	T.H. White	Jacobs	*Beauty and the Beast*	*Peter Pan*
Norse	C.S. Lewis	Beowulf	Le Guin	Perrault	Later Andersen	E. Nesbit
Hebrew	Tolkien	Arthurian	*Superman*	Grimm	Wilde	Ghost stories
H	**I**	**J**	**K**	**L**	**M**	**N**
Treasure Island	*Jane Eyre*	E. Blyton	*The Secret Garden*	Very few	Southall	(Animals, toys etc.)
Joan Aiken	*Lord of the*	Holiday and	*A Little Princess*	examples?	Naughton	Potter
War comics	*Flies*	school	True love stories		E.J. Keats	Hoban
	Sutcliff	adventures				

At no point does Warlow suggest that this is a chart that classifies texts exhaustively (see page 128). It is an application of a way of sorting texts that shows how some historic categories, such as 'myth' and 'legend', can be understood. There are two particular points about the chart that make it valuable. First, it has found some of the significant distinctions that can subdivide a collection of children's books. These include the maintenance or suspension of the laws of nature, the centrality of action or feeling and the various settings he locates. Within the chart there are some of the critical generic categories that subdivide children's literature. Secondly, the chart has concentrated on the content of stories. In his work on the teaching of writing Cairney (1995) raises the anxiety that much work on genre could 'place form and structure before meaning'. Warlow has drawn on the content of the stories as the raw material for this classification but, as he makes clear in his question about books such as *Tarka the Otter* and *Rupert Bear* (see page 127), it is not a superficial focus upon content. Instead it finds significant similarities within a genre.

IN PRACTICE: GENRE

The use of genre as a tool for selection and its impact upon the reader's expectations are examples of the ways in which the developing grasp of this area of literary theory is operative in many readers. The classification of stories draws on the understanding of some sort of familial resemblance between a group of texts. These reading behaviours can be enhanced by activities that develop the child's understanding of genre. The learning objectives underpinning such activities are that children should learn to:

✧ understand the sort of generic resemblances that indicate the identity of a particular genre group;

✧ classify texts using their own understanding of genre;

✧ develop an awareness of the various uses of genre.

Activities that foster such objectives include the following suggestions.

THE TERM 'GENRE'

As with so many of the terms used in this book, the term 'genre' is one children can be introduced to from a very young age. Teachers will often discuss 'similar sorts of books' or talk to a child about 'the sort of book you enjoy' when there is a ready-made term that could often cover the same ground. The earlier the term 'genre' is used, the earlier children will become accustomed to its use.

SPIDERGRAMS

What ideas does the name of a particular genre evoke? Genres are not subdivided by one simple trait. A murder does not automatically make a story a piece of crime fiction. If it did we would have to class *Macbeth* and *Arsenic and Old Lace* in the same family. Genres develop through a conglomeration of images and events cropping up in various stories. This idea can be used in a simple spidergram. A genre title is placed at the centre of a piece of paper and children cluster ideas that they associate with the genre around that title. For example, a group of Year 1 children working on the title 'fairy tale' came up with this range of comments.

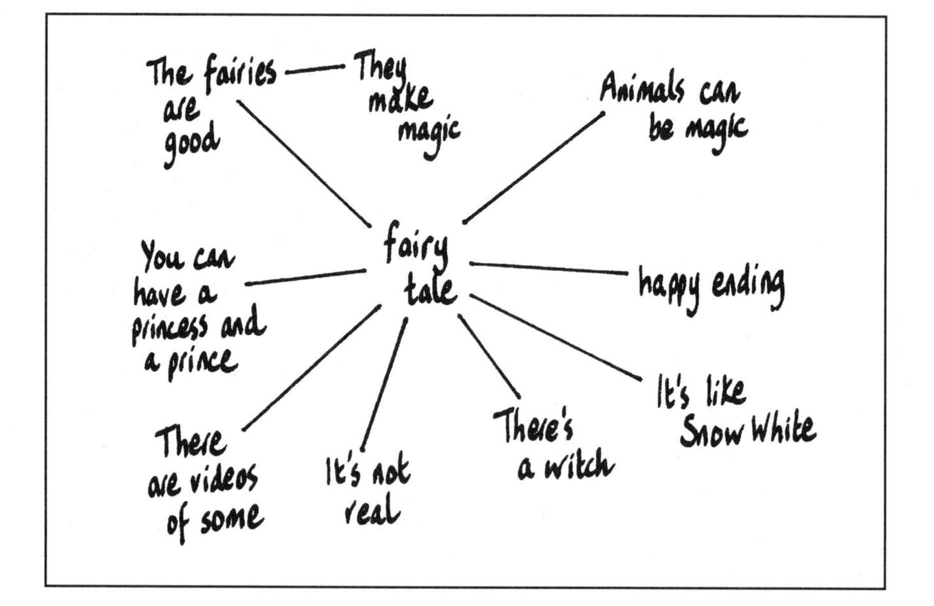

Many just named a story in the category (for example, 'like 'Snow White'). Other comments showed common traits (for example, 'They make magic', 'It's not real', 'happy ending').

Older children could also look at this genre, digging deeper into the commonality between texts to discern the familial resemblance. They could notice the similarity of characters featured in such stories or the prevalence of the 'rule of three' (by which there are often three repetitions of, for example, Rumpelstiltskin's visits to the girl, the soldier's following of twelve dancing princesses, Jack's trips up the beanstalk). A genre such as 'science fiction' will evoke an entirely different set of expectations. Any genre can lend itself to drawing out of children the traits they commonly associate with it.

REALISTIC AND FANTASTIC

Children can look through the stock of books that make up the book corner or the reading scheme and classify the stories using Warlow's idea of a story's 'similarity or dissimilarity to the external world as we see it and generally understand it'.

Three piles are made: the 'realistic', the 'fantastic' and the 'undecided'. The reasons children present for putting texts into the various piles can be interesting. For example, children can do odd things, such as collecting all stories linked to the distant medieval and prehistoric past in the 'fantastic' pile, even those that show no departure from the normal laws of nature. As with sequencing activities, the end result is interesting but much of the learning takes place in the reasoning that goes into creating the three piles.

One note of caution. It is worth stressing before the children start the activity that the three piles do not consist of the 'true' story and the 'made-up' story. What is being distinguished is the difference between stories they believe could have happened and those that could not. This can be an interesting distinction for young children to make – I can recall one seven-year-old telling me, 'I know there's a Father Christmas because I've seen the film.'

FIVE FAMILIES

This activity is very much like the previous one but it engages children with the task of compiling their own criteria for subdividing stories. For the activity, a group of children need a selection of about 30 books. It is preferable if they are familiar with the stories. It can be a stock of books they have read from nursery age. Alternatively, reading-scheme books can be a useful resource for this because they are often quickly read! The books need to be varied in subject matter.

The task is to group the books into four or five families. Some guidance can be given such as, 'Put stories that are like each other into a family,' but it is important to leave open the grounds for grouping stories together.

Once the grouping is done, the children can give the piles family names and write down what each family grouping has in common. (For example, 'The monster family: all the books have got a monster in them', 'The problem family: in these stories there is trouble!')

An interesting follow-up can involve listing the family names and the texts grouped into each family, then jumbling the books up again and asking a different group of children to repeat the exercise with the same texts. Once they have completed the exercise the two sets of results can be compared. It can reveal some interesting similarities and differences in how the two groups classified the texts.

USES OF GENRE

Children can locate and note examples of genre in use. Uses such as the classification sometimes used in school and children's libraries and the classification of sections in video shops provide examples in the environment.

In television guides the films are often collected and listed separately. These can be scanned, looking for some of the genres used to subdivide such works. Examples such as 'film noir', 'kitchen-sink drama' and 'swashbuckler' are interesting because they tend to be used solely to classify films.

The publisher's blurb on the back of novels can also contain an indication of the genre. The blurb on the back of Helen Cresswell's *The Watchers* includes the following text:

> And there, in that other world, Katy and Josh meet goodness and evil and discover the terrifying mystery of Alton Towers.

The word 'mystery' gives some indication of the territory the reader can expect to be in in this book.

THE CHALLENGE OF A RANGE OF TEXTS

There is much to be commended in the range of stories that features in the contemporary primary curriculum. However, some of the requirements present a challenge to teachers who may be unfamiliar with the type of story being recommended. The range of literature available presents several challenges:

- ✧ the need to develop a good working collection of stories from a range of cultures;
- ✧ the need to find, within the long established fiction that is available, the texts that will work in a modern classroom;
- ✧ the need to engage children with the work of 'significant children's authors' in a way that looks at their texts but also develops the child's awareness of the author.

What follows are some suggestions for covering this range.

STORIES FROM A RANGE OF CULTURES

A collection such as Michael Rosen's *South and North, East and West* (1992) demonstrates the wealth of stories available from different cultures. It is crucial that we develop the awareness of children so that they see the range of cultures that are rich sources of stories.

DEVELOPING A SCHOOL COLLECTION OF STORIES

The collection should encompass many different types of story (for example, myths, fables) from a wide range of cultural backgrounds and should contain material for all age groups. The principal focus of this collection should be to provide a resource that is culturally diverse. It is important to test out the material filed away in such a collection, and the aim is not to amass an exhaustive archive but rather a selective resource that covers a wide cultural range. Few things are more unappealing and useless to a teacher than the sight of a file of unused photocopies. It is best to be ruthlessly selective and only retain the tried and tested.

FIND A TELLER

Many stories lie dead on the page because their genre is that of an orally told folk tale. The phrases and dialects that often add the extra magic to such tales can only be fully enjoyed if such stories are heard. Local libraries or arts groups can often provide contact numbers for storytellers. Children themselves can demonstrate a brilliance at retelling stories, an ability to be fostered.

CHILDREN AS COLLECTORS

The idea of a resource that collects stories together, ensuring they are heard and read rather than lost, can be an exciting one for children. They can often be encouraged to explore their own cultures collecting their own life stories. The school can also collect local 'urban myths' and pieces of local history. Such a collecting activity clarifies the fact that we all have a culture from which we can draw stories.

LONG-ESTABLISHED TEXTS

The thought of reading a 'classic' leads to a part of the reading range many teachers wish to avoid. The idea of reading a book like *Children of the New Forest* often does not go down well with today's practitioner. Such texts can be lengthy and full of drawn-out descriptive passages. Teachers will often be uncomfortable at some of the Victorian moralising in such stories. However, the idea of stories having a long and varied history is an important one. Furthermore it is surprising how enduring some texts are, for example Frances Hodgson Burnett's *A Little Princess* (1905) or Oscar Wilde's *The Selfish Giant* (1888). The following points may be of use in planning to work with older texts.

SHORT CAN BE BEAUTIFUL

Short stories can provide a way into older texts. Some of the short stories of E. Nesbit or the fairy stories of Oscar Wilde can provide a reading experience short enough to maintain a child's interest. Stories like *The Happy Prince* by Oscar Wilde (1888) are still very popular among children.

WHY READ IT ALL?

Some stories can ramble in places and lose the child's interest. Subtleties in the text can be missed by young readers. However, in cases such as these there is the age-old method of reading – skipping – which can be done successfully with a little forethought. Passages can be chosen that will work well for reading in class, a summary of what happens between the selected passages being given for continuity.

DRAW UPON AUDIO AND VISUAL INTERPRETATIONS

Tapes of stories, often edited versions to fit the cassette, can provide a way into such texts. Videos can also make stories accessible. Some lengthy classics have been produced as films. Watching these in conjunction with reading portions of the original novel is one way of handling such texts.

SIGNIFICANT AUTHORS

The requirement to read modern fiction by significant children's authors raises the exciting possibility that children can develop a taste for the work of a particular author. When this happens it can have a significant effect on the amount of reading a child will pursue. You only have to look at the success of the works of R.L. Stine, author of the 'Goosebumps' titles, to get some idea of the potential pull a particular author's name can have. The following suggestions are aimed at developing the interest of individual children in the works of particular authors.

CORRESPONDENCE

Children can be encouraged to write to particular authors or their publishers or agents. Authors can sometimes be a disappointment and it pays to check with the publisher as to the kind of response children can expect to receive before starting on the letter writing. Some writers take great pains to reply to many, if not all, of the correspondents they hear from. Certain publishers will often send advertising posters featuring particular authors and their work.

VISITS FROM AUTHORS

Many authors visit schools. Here again, there is the need to be guarded. An author may be sparky and go down well with children on the page but there is no guarantee that he or she won't be a complete bore at a face-to-face meeting. It is worth trying to get recommendations from other schools that have used an author before you embark on arranging a visit. They often charge a fee but it can be well worth every penny.

ABOUT THE AUTHOR

Collecting material about particular authors can be an interesting way of developing interest in their work. I have worked with Key Stage 1 children using a video of Jill Murphy as a stimulus before reading through a collection of her books. Having seen her at work with colouring pencils, the class started to take great interest in the shades and colours in her illustrations.

Magazines such as *Books for Keeps* feature interviews with children's authors. There is also the blurb on the back cover of many books providing information about the author. A number of children's publishers are now adopting a policy of making these pieces child orientated.

AN EXPANDING RANGE

There is a sense in which genres make literature accessible. They give the reader a picture of the sorts of texts that are available, what is new on the market, what the reader has tried before and enjoyed, and so on. For the teacher they provide a way of working with the range of texts we want our children to read. They have also enabled schools to plan for a more innovative reading experience, covering a wider historical and cultural range of texts than might otherwise have been used.

Genres are artificial categories. But like many artificial categories, they have evolved because they serve a useful purpose. An understanding of genre will enable children to map their experience of stories, making them aware of where they have still to travel.

CHAPTER 6

READER RESPONSE THEORY

Reading is a creative act. I sat down and wrote the words you are now reading. If you didn't read these words then their meaning would come to nothing. There is a sense in which the meaning of what I write will not exist unless you carry out the creative task of making sense of what I have written. A whole body of theory and criticism has grown up around this role of the reader in the making of meaning.

The National Curriculum programme of study for Reading at Key Stage 2 specifically mentions this aspect of the reading curriculum, requiring that pupils *'...should be encouraged to respond imaginatively to the plot, characters, ideas, vocabulary and organisation of language in literature. They should be taught to use inference and deduction'*.

At Key Stage 1 the programme of study refers to children *'understanding and responding to stories'* and recommends that the material read should include *'interesting subject matter and settings, which may be related to pupils' own experience or extend beyond their knowledge of the everyday'*.

This chapter looks at the work of theorists who have emphasised the importance of the reader's response in the reading of texts. For these theorists it is not just a part of the process of reading, it is fundamental to the act of making sense of a text and grasping its meaning. What is being examined is the way we can work alongside the very act of reading. The section 'The text: looking at what readers read' focuses on the text and the ways readers can look at the text to develop an understanding of their response to it. The third section focuses on readers reflecting on themselves, looking at who is responding. The final section suggests some ways of developing the recording of responses.

The practical suggestions in this chapter are placed within the theoretical sections; there is no clear switch between the two. The reason for this is that this chapter, more than any other, brings the theory and practice together in the act of reading and responding.

RESPONSE AND MEANING

A number of theorists and ideas cluster together under this umbrella of reader response theory. They share an emphasis on the role of the reader in the creation of meaning. One such theorist, Stanley Fish (1970), entitled an essay 'Literature in the Reader', a clear statement that the meaning of the text resides in the activity of the reader. He opens the essay addressing that reader:

> If at this moment someone were to ask, 'what are you doing?' you might reply 'I am reading,' and thereby acknowledge the fact that reading is an activity, something *you do*. No one would argue that the act of reading can take place in the absence of someone who reads - how can you tell the dance from the dancer?' (page 70)

Though they differ in many ways, Fish's fellow reader-response theorist, Wolfgang Iser (1980), presents the act of reading in equally prosaic terms. The image he uses to illustrate the role of the reader who reads the literary work is to consider the literary work as having two poles. One of these can be termed the *artistic*. This pole is the author's text. It is tempting to regard this, in itself, as the literary work. However, Iser fills out the picture by placing the realisation of the text by the reader at an opposite pole which he labels the *aesthetic*. He suggests that the literary work 'cannot be identical with the text or with its actualisation but must be situated somewhere between the two' (page 106).

Iser points to the interaction between any two people communicating with each other. I can't know all your experience and you can't know all mine. As we communicate we make contact, form views, react to one another, all of which works on the gap that is between us: 'Contact therefore depends upon our continually filling in a central gap in our experience' (page 108).

There are obvious differences between communicating with a person individually and reading a text. If you were talking on the phone to me at this moment you could stop me right here and say, 'I understand...' or, 'Hang on a minute,' and so on. But there is one significant similarity. Our interaction in conversation forms that gap-filling process because we are different people with different experiences. To communicate with each other involves filling in the gap. Iser suggests there is a similarity when we read:

> ...it is the gaps, the fundamental asymmetry between text and reader, that give rise to communication in the reading process... (page 109)

As teachers, a large part of our work is taken up with the dynamics of reading. Over the past 20 or so years there has been a so-called 'Great Debate' about the way in which children learn to read which has quite rightly directed a lot of time and energy to looking at the various strategies children use for processing words on a page. In working on the reader's response we are complementing the work done on the process of decoding the words on the page with a further look at what the young reader learns to make of those words. The fact remains that there are an alarming number of fluent readers who are turned off reading. Many teachers will have experienced working with children who, while they can read fiction – for them the decoding process is not a problem – are what we could call 'unresponsive' to it. What is needed is a development of the response they make to a text. Martin and Leather (1994) offer the following advice on what is needed to make a reader.

> In order to become a reader, you first have to have an experience which affects you powerfully. Then you want it again. Before long you are hooked and cannot do without a regular fix. (page 7)

Our work as teachers needs to extend beyond the initial decoding skills to engaging with children on their response to stories. Reader response theory can direct us towards the task readers undertake with the processed words. It will lead to children reflecting on their response to those words.

THE TEXT: LOOKING AT WHAT READERS READ

Returning to Iser's image of the artistic and the aesthetic as two poles, the actual literary work occurs between these two poles. That image opens up some interesting possibilities for exploration. It gives an insight into the process of reading that can inform our task as teachers and opens the possibility of exploring this area of the reader's response with the young readers in our class. In this section we start with the artistic pole, taking a look at what readers work on as they make sense of a text. This is done with a view towards targeting the objectives that children learn to:

✧ examine the way the whole text and parts of a text work together;
✧ work with complex texts in which the meaning is open to varied interpretations;
✧ follow the way the unfolding of a story affects the reader's response;
✧ focus on significant features of language and illustration and the effect these have on their response to a text;
✧ make inferences that fill the gaps in a text.

These objectives will enable readers to look at features of the text that encourage or enable a particular response.

It is important to bear two things in mind when working through this list of textual features. Firstly, any look at a reader's response will inevitably be 'after the fact'. If someone comes up to you now, points at this book and says, 'Any good?' you will stop reading and answer. You will stop reading and verbalise your response, but the actual process of responding takes place now as you read these words. Any discussion or exploration of how you understood something meaningful in a text takes place after you did it. As Culler (in Freund, 1987) remarks, 'To speak of the meaning of a work is to tell a story of reading' (page 87).

Secondly, the list of features that prompts response is artificially subdivided in order to help in the understanding of facets of a text that, in reality, work as one. Such subdivisions are purely for the purposes of examining ideas and to sharpen our focus. With this in mind we can now take a look at some of the artificially subdivided entities that are encountered and responded to.

A. THE TEXT: PARTS AND WHOLE

As we read we have a tendency to piece together the different parts into a whole. We recognise the roles and actions of different actants, we see the causal links between things that happen. We develop what Culler (1981) calls *models of unity*. We relate the various parts of our reading to an overall interpretation.

We interpret the parts of a text in the light of our model of unity. At the same time our understanding of the parts of the text causes us to develop and revise that model. It is a circular process.

In *Rumpelstiltskin*, when a goblin enters the room of the princess who is trying to spin straw into gold the common response – that is, this is a story about an evil goblin – will be suspended by his apparent helpfulness in a desperate situation. The whole story thus far will influence our response to the goblin. When he later tries to take the princess's child away the reader will revise this interpretation of what is going on in the whole story and see him as the enemy. Our understanding of the whole story causes us to sympathise with the girl. The way these parts build up the whole picture and create the context for the understanding of the parts involves a complex relationship; it is a circular relationship made up of two components: the parts, which relate to the whole, and the whole, which is made up of parts.

PARTS RELATE TO THE WHOLE

In our reading with children it is important to nurture their development of models of unity. We need to encourage them to keep their eye on the way the whole story is developing. Once they have grasped the mechanics of decoding the words on the page or once they are attentively listening to the stories we read, we need to develop this relationship between the parts and the whole. If we are to take children from the early stages of picture books to the reading of longer novels this will be crucial.

A novel such as Ridley's *Krindlekrax* has so many twists and turns, recounting the past, using symbolism and foreshadowing the future, that it becomes easy for children to run along the text or take in each episode of each day's story reading and completely miss the point of the whole story. Many teachers will have had the experience of the child who can read texts fluently, decoding the words, but has little idea of what is going on in the story. The skills of reading alone do not provide the ability to maintain a holistic interpretation of the story.

The teacher can help to develop this model of unity. On finishing a picture book you can pick out the main joke or theme in the story. When returning to a story in which the reading is being serialised, the recap on 'what happened last time we read' needs to be supplemented by a couple of points about how the whole of what has been read so far is fitting together.

Developing such models of unity can be a major factor in combating the boredom that can infect a child's reading of longer texts. If the children are missing the point of a story their enthusiasm is bound to flag. In Catherine Fisher's *The Snow*

Walker's Son a major part of the first half of the story involves the central characters going on a long journey (taking up 59 pages). This section of the story propels the action towards the confrontation with the much feared 'Snow Walker's Son'. It is exactly the sort of narrative passage that can lead a child to lose interest. The story is excellent but if the reader has missed the point of the suspense generated by the travellers' fear as they approach the confrontation with the 'Snow Walker's Son' then these chapters offer little more than a gathering of people walking through the snow. The anticipation is an essential part of the whole story. Developing a grasp of the whole creates the overall interpretation that fuels the reading of the parts.

WHOLE MADE UP OF THE PARTS

The other component of this circle involves the way in which our overall reading makes us monitor the parts. A seemingly straightforward modern picture book such as Martin Waddell's *The Tough Princess* (1986) involves a fantastic and complex interplay of parts. The king and queen hatch a scheme to become rich by having a daughter and getting her into trouble with a bad fairy. They plan that a prince will rescue her. In the end, the bad fairy is beaten up by the princess. The princess rescues the prince instead of the prince rescuing her. It works extremely well, the whole story being made up of many subtle and unexpected parts.

When it comes to identifying and discussing the constituent parts of a whole story the primary teacher is on to a winner. A class of 30 children will often answer a question such as, 'What was the best part of the story?' or 'What happened in the story?' with an array of answers, with individual children making different points about different parts of the text. In working towards developing a model of unity, this variety can be welcomed as a way of children showing one another the diverse responses they are making to the same text.

An interesting way I have seen of working with this diversity involved a large ball of string. The children were sitting on the carpet in a group giving responses to the story, picking out parts they liked, questions they had and so on. The first child made his response. Another child followed on from this response, so the string was unrolled from the first child to the second. Another child followed on, so it was rolled on to her. By the end of the session the class were sitting in a web on the carpet. They then had to roll the ball of string back up, remembering what each of them had pointed out as the string passed their way. Not only did it result in a recall of the different responses but it also visibly demonstrated how the various parts of the text were woven together into the whole story.

B. THE TEXT: OPEN TEXTS

Some texts are more demanding than others. Some stories are easier to follow. It's the difference between James Joyce and Jeffery Archer. This difference between texts affects our response as readers. In his work on *The Role of the Reader* (1979) Umberto Eco distinguishes between *closed* and *open* texts. A closed text is a straightforward story that gives the reader a reasonably clear path to follow as he or she interprets what is going on. It could also be said that it restricts the responses we can make and gives little latitude for a variety of creative responses. He cites the example of Superman comic strips.

> They apparently aim at pulling the reader along a predetermined path, carefully displaying their effects so as to arouse pity or fear, excitement or depression at the due place and at the right moment. (page 8)

In contrast, an open text is marked by a complexity that offers opportunities for a range of interpretations by the reader. The complexity defies an easy read. To quote Eco again, the ideal reader for an open text will be 'affected by an ideal insomnia... eager to deal with the text as with a maze of many issues' (page 9).

Although this openness can prove demanding, like a path that is not predetermined, the enjoyment or fascination of such texts can lie in that very openness. There is something richer in the opening line of Dylan Thomas's poem to his dying father (1952), 'Do not go gentle into that good night', than if he had just said, 'Don't die quietly.' The demand is not on the reader's decoding of the text but on the task of making sense of what is read.

Before we look at the way we as teachers can work with such open texts, it is worth pointing out that the distinction between closed and open texts is not a straight alternative. Like many distinctions in literary theory this isn't a clean-cut split. Green and LeBihan (1996) point out that:

> ...this is not a straightforward binarism, and it is better to think of the difference operating in degrees rather than being one of kind. (page 205)

OPEN TEXTS WITH CHILDREN

When Michael Rosen writes about Big Tony in the narrative poem 'Go-kart' (1983) he tells us that:

> Big Tony was terrific
> because Big Tony told us he was.

Because Big Tony was *very* big he was big enough to tell everyone just that, without any arguments. He also drove his go-kart with admirable flair. At this point Rosen could have stated the simple fact, 'I was jealous of big Tony.' But the poem gives us additional information. What the poem tells us is:

> I was jealous of Big Tony.
> I was afraid that I thought
> he might be
> terrific.

The second, third and fourth lines mean that we suddenly have something that is more complex. Jealousy may not be as straightforward as we first thought. These lines demand that the reader works a little bit harder to make sense of the text, but it is worth the work.

In his story *The Lamplighter's Funeral* (1984) Leon Garfield depicts a cold, hard world in which a Georgian lamplighter, Pallcat, takes in an apprentice, Possul. The old lamplighter's only real pleasure is stitching biblical texts on the theme of light. He puts the apprentice to bed and:

> For an hour or so after Possul was asleep, Pallcat stitched away at his unfinished text, which was always his bedtime pleasure and task and somehow made his world seem larger...

In the above example, Garfield's text is open. The reader is not dragged along a straightforward statement (such as 'Pallcat thoroughly enjoyed stitching his texts'). The meaning of the line that says that the task 'somehow made his world seem larger' is open for us to make our sense of what it says.

The open line, paragraph or page, providing a more challenging text demanding that much more from the reader, can be an example of Meek's idea of the text teaching the reader how to read. This is noticeable in a number of picture books whose language belies any notion of their simplicity. In Dyan Sheldon's and Gary Blythe's *The Garden* (1993) Jenny sleeps outside and encounters American Indians from the past. They tell her about the past and about a time

> When there were stories in the stars and songs in the sun.
> When everything on earth had a voice and a heart, and time was measured by the changings of the moon.

This sort of depth of language isn't uncommon in children's books.

MAKING THE MOST OF THE OPEN TEXT

Generally, the instinct of a young reader is to scoot over a text following the action. Working with texts or parts of texts that are more demanding involves promoting them and thereby promoting the sort of reading they demand. The more open parts of texts can be re-read, much in the way that poems are often re-read for the same sort of richness. This can involve opening up discussion for children to share what they understand from the text. Chunks of text can be printed out and copied and children can be encouraged to read them in a whole-class shared reading session. Alternatively, individuals may choose to take the texts and read them individually. I remember one struggling reader who worked on the opening lines of Ted Hughes's *The Iron Man* (1968). He learned the words and chose to re-read them daily for a couple of weeks. He recited them aloud, 'turning over' the words, enjoying them and loving their language.

Above all, the challenge of open texts should push us to consider the texts we read to our classes. Storytime isn't a filler between afternoon break and hometime. It should be an essential part of a child's introduction to reading throughout his or her school life.

The whole-class read is the ideal context for tackling challenging stories. For example, I have read Michael Ende's *The Neverending Story* with a Year 3 class. I am sure that its complexity would have swamped any one of those children if they had set out to read it alone but as a class reader it was manageable. I took a Year 2 class through the bizarre Russell Hoban story *The Marzipan Pig* (1986). Here again, it worked because we worked on it together.

What amazes me is the number of classrooms, particularly at Key Stage 2, in which the whole class storytime is being abandoned. Storytime provides *the* opportunity to introduce children to texts in which the demands made on the reader are matched by the rewards of the passage. Take the following extract from Ende, for example.

> ...the second gate will be there for you. The Magic Mirror Gate... when you stand before it, you see yourself. But not as you would in an ordinary mirror. You don't see your outward appearance; what you see is your real innermost nature. If you want to go through, you have to – in a manner of speaking – go into yourself.

C. THE TEXT: HAPPENINGS

Reading is a process. Something happens as readers read. This creative act involves reading bit by bit and tying together the things that are read. Stanley Fish (1976) uses the following lines from Milton to show one of the ways in which meanings in readings can seem neatly resolved, only to come undone. What the reader needs to do is to read the quote below line by line. Place a piece of paper over it, letting it slip down a line at a time. At the end of each line you should ask yourself what you have found out so far.

> The willows and the hazel copses green
> Shall now no more be seen,
> Fanning their joyous leaves to thy soft lays.

After the first two lines we seem to have been told that the willows and copses won't be seen any more. In Fish's words: '...at the end of line 43 [the second line] the reader will have hazarded an interpretation, or performed an act of perceptual closure...' (page 164). However, that interpretation proves wrong when we find that the next line defines how, in future, the willows and copses will not be seen; it is simply that they will not be 'fanning their joyous leaves'. Fish explains that, whatever the reader has done at the end of line 43, he or she 'will undo it in the act of reading the next line'.

In this example something happens to the reader or listener. We assume we have the meaning all tied up, only to find it unravelling. We then have to revise our understanding of the text. In Tony Ross's *I'm Coming to Get You*, a monster hurtles

through space destroying whole planets before picking up little Tommy Brown on its radar. As he comes closer to Earth the monster maintains the refrain, 'I'm coming to get you'. The common assumption is that this is a classic scenario, big monster coming after little human. As Tommy sets off for school the next day the monster pounces. The common assumption must then be revised. The monster is pictured and is, in fact, smaller than Tommy's shoe.

The responses we make alter as we read. Some stories capitalise on this in the way that they surprise the reader, for example in Munsch's *The Paper Bag Princess* (1982) in which the princess saves a prince and then ditches him when he criticises her appearance. In Tony Ross's *Oscar Got the Blame* (1987) the reader witnesses Oscar's attempts to blame all the naughty things that happen around the house on his imaginary friend Billy. On the penultimate page he is sent to his room complaining that, 'It's not fair!... Nobody believes in my friend Billy'. The story closes with a picture of an evil-looking child leaping around with the words, '"They never do!" said Billy'.

Instead of discussing the story at the end we can sometimes make more of stories like these by discussing them just before the end. The interpretations of 'the story so far' can be collected before a launch into their undoing. (If you do pause in this way before the ending it pays to backtrack a page or two when you return to the story. This makes the most of the way in which such stories flow so well into the final moment.)

'BUT' STATEMENTS

The word 'but' can be a useful resource. To make 'but' statements, children can be given a starter sentence such as 'I want to be a good kid', 'School is great' or 'I love going to bed early'. What they have to do is put a 'but' at the end of the sentence, then finish it off (for example, 'I want to be a good kid *but not just yet*', 'School is great *but only when it's closed*' or 'I love going to bed early *but only when I decide to myself*'). The simple pattern is to build up, then knock down, an expectation.

GOOD/BAD TALES

Good/bad tales are part of our oral culture. In these narrative doggerels the first line presents a good scenario but it is scotched by the next line. The poem 'Two Pilots', adapted by Michael Rosen (1987), starts like this:

> Two pilots went up in an aeroplane
> The aeroplane had a good engine.
> That's good.
> No, that's bad. The engine stopped.
> Oh, that's bad.
> No, they had parachutes.
> Oh, that's good.
> No, that was bad – the parachutes
> didn't open.

This idea can be used in group storytelling. Children devise a story that involves a character in a chain of events that are good and bad alternately. Initially they will often just add an unlinked bad event to a good event. One child says, 'They got married and lived in a palace,' and another child follows on with, 'A crocodile ate them.' They can often get the hang of picking up something from the good event and making it bad. So one child can say, 'They got married and lived in a palace,' the next child then taking the idea of the palace and using it: 'The palace collapsed while they were in it.' It is an artificial method of exploring the way in which our response alters as we make sense of a text by swinging the balance of fortune and misfortune in our own story.

The twists and turns in a narrative play a critical part in our enjoyment of the text. Whether it be that moment when the Stone Table cracks and the children in Narnia discover that Aslan is alive or the final scene in the airport at the end of *Casablanca*, stories are riddled with these abrupt changes that add so much to their pleasure. If we can demonstrate this to children it will further encourage their response.

D. THE TEXT: LANGUAGE

Read the following pieces of language, pause after each line and try to gauge what sorts of feelings or experiences each of them evokes in you. Show the words to a colleague and see how your reactions differ:

> dentist
> the Prime Minister
> compromise
> sprouts

No two people will respond in the same way to that list. We will all have different reactions to the word 'dentist'. Reactions to the term 'Prime Minister' will vary depending on who he or she is. The vagaries of a word like 'compromise' will throw open a breadth of possible reactions. And there may even be someone out there who read 'sprouts' and thought 'yummy'.

The theorist Norman Holland (1980) looked at the varied responses readers give to the use of the word 'fathered' in one line of a William Faulkner story. Different readers presented a range of responses. Holland considered that range with the observation:

> ...since the text presents just the one word 'fathered', one cannot explain by means of the text alone why one reader would find that word heroic, another neutral and abstract, and a third sexual... At the Center for the Psychological Study of the Arts, we have found that we can explain such differences in interpretation by examining differences in the personalities of the interpreters. More precisely, *interpretation is a function of identity*... (page 123)

Responses to the language of the text will vary from reader to reader. Looking at the language of the text and the way in which readers respond to it can provide a focus for exploring responses.

There are several ways in which teachers can provide opportunities for recording responses to the language of a text. The following are a few suggestions:

MARGINS

If children are provided with copies of a piece of text with a wide margin down the side, they can write their responses to parts of the text, drawing arrows to point to the words on which they are commenting. For instance, you can ask them to point out words that develop mystery, describe a setting or develop their impression of a particular character. Take, for example, the first few pages of Ross's *Super Dooper Jezebel*:

> Jezebel was perfect in every way. She was so perfect she was called Super Dooper Jezebel.
>
> When other children came out of school, they were sometimes untidy, but Jezebel was always super dooper neat.
>
> Jezebel always kept her room tidy, and she always put her things back in their boxes...
> and she cleaned up after the cat.

In this example the children could be asked to point out, circle or highlight the four words or phrases that say the most about Jezebel, such as 'perfect in every way', 'neat', 'kept her room tidy' and 'cleaned up after the cat'. More able writers can point out four words or phrases that they think describe Jezebel and also jot down in the margin what those words make them think of. This may be something from their own experience, for example 'My room is never tidy'.

USING THE OHP

Overhead projector images also provide a way of looking at a piece of text together. If these are projected on to an A1 sheet of paper, children can pick out favourite lines or phrases and they or the teacher can mark the text, allowing for a group to collate responses on one large sheet. This can involve the sorts of responses recorded in the last suggestion, and the teacher can also model examples on such a text. If you take, for example, the description of a character in a text and work on it in this way, it will add a visual dimension to the types of discussions of character we looked at in Chapter 2.

WORD POOLS

Word pools provide a way of identifying the crucial words in a limited piece of text. The children are provided with a shared text, photocopied, in a big book or on an overhead projection. They then have to decide which words are the most significant in the text, working in pairs. They then draw a pool shape on a piece of paper and decide which words to select from the text to put in it. The example below shows a word pool which draws significant words and phrases from *The Snow Maze*.

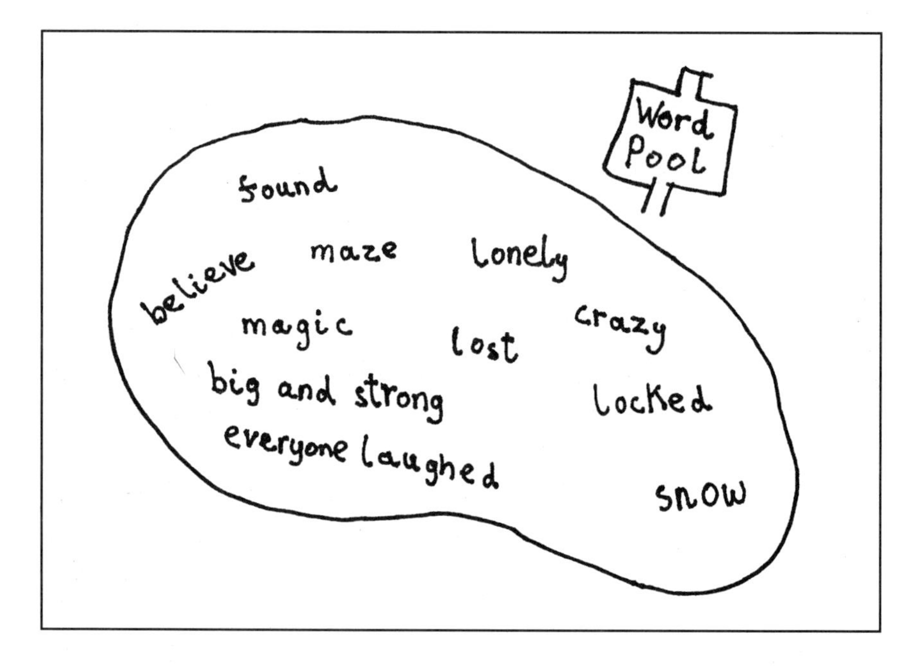

WORD RESPONSE

Responses can be collected to one word or phrase that will feature in a story before you read it. For example, before

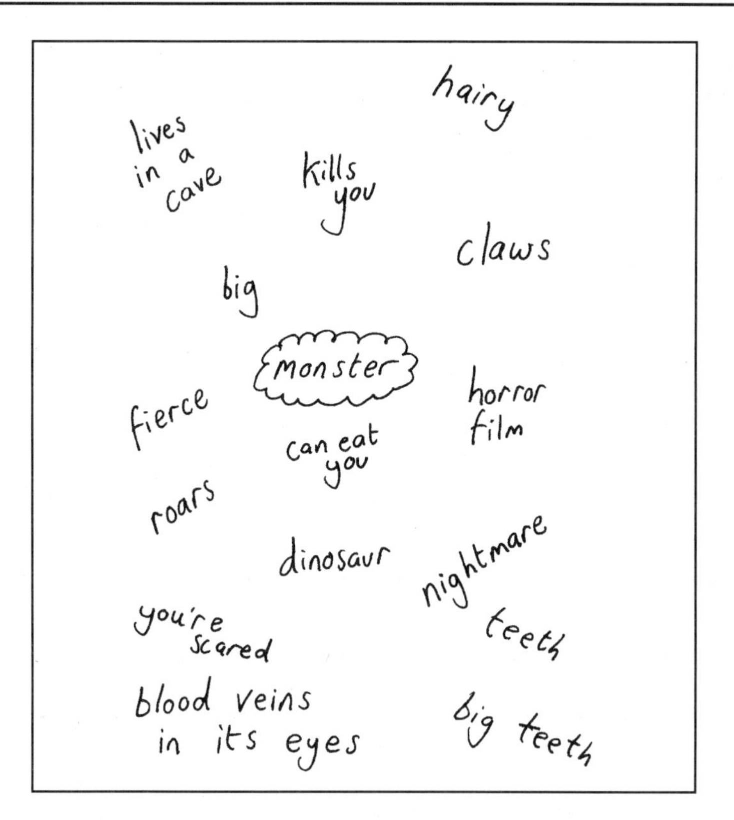

watching a performance of *A Midsummer Night's Dream*, ask the children what thoughts the word 'forest' or 'fairy' brings to their minds. Or before reading *I'm Coming to Get You* collect their reactions to the word 'monster'.

A brainstorming chart can illustrate the varied responses. This will produce a more effective end-product if the children are asked to first think of their initial responses and jot them down. These can then be collated on to one chart. It is worth starting the activity by collecting responses individually, otherwise children can sometimes latch on to the ideas of the first two contributors and simply rephrase them, so that the chart ends up with the words 'It is big', 'It is large', 'It is enormous' and so on. The responses are supposed to vary because they are personal. If they have been jotted down beforehand it will result in a much more interesting sharing of personal responses.

As a teacher you will find that with the texts you know best you will develop a good idea of the words that will provide a good focus for this activity. The responses recorded on such lists or brainstorms can be reviewed after going through the story to look at how the children's interaction with the text may have modified their responses to the word or phrase that they were given before the reading of the story.

COLLOCATION

The use of a particular word close to other words (*collocation*) can affect our response. In Roald Dahl's *Matilda* (1988) there are 63 occasions when her father is referred to with a preceding 'the' (that is, 'the father'). This form of reference influences our response to his personality. The alternative is the loving parent in Dahl's *Danny the Champion of the World* (1975). Of that book's 365 uses of the word 'father', 354 use the collocate 'my', as in 'my father' (Knowles and Malmkjaer, 1996).

Flick through a chapter of any book looking at the words that are collocated with a particular name or place. This can often show the way in which the language influences our response as readers. In Eva Ibbotson's *The Secret of Platform 13* (1994) the unlikeable child, Raymond, features in Chapter 7, wriggling, staring, shouting, shuddering, shrieking – all of which develop our response to his character. Re-reading a chapter or a story and collecting the words that occur close to a character's name or the name of a place can provide an inventory of the language that influences response.

OCCURRENCE

It is worth pointing out and sometimes even keeping track of the number of times a word or phrase is used in one text. Sometimes there is a clear top of the poll, as in Millar's *On Your Potty* (1991) in which Baby Ba's ten uses of the word 'Nah' in refusing to go on his potty dominate the text. It is the sort of phrase many infant teachers will be used to, the one in which the children chime in with the reading of the text. It's like the refrain of Tony Ross's monster, 'I'm coming to get you!' in the story of the same name.

This lacing of a text with a crucial word or phrase supports our shared reading of texts with younger children as they join in with the repetition. It is also a feature of texts children can emulate in their own story writing. They can be asked to think of their own repeated phrases for inclusion in a story (for example, 'You can't make me!', 'It's boring' or, in a more positive light, 'I thought that was a great idea' or simply 'Yes, yes, yes!' – the scope for appropriately chosen inclusions that are used repetitively is limitless!).

E. THE TEXT: DESIGN AND ILLUSTRATION

Much of the literature we deal with in the primary classroom contains more than just the written text. In developing the responses of the children we work with we need to give a high profile to the role illustration and design play in many of the books we use.

A classic example is Pat Hutchins's book *Rosie's Walk*. The text is very simple. It is just 'Rosie the hen went for a walk', followed by the places she walked past. The text is complemented by the illustrations in which the fox is shown making unsuccessful attempts to catch the hen. The text does not stand alone. The reader has to make use of the illustrations.

Extreme examples of the employment of this technique are stories such as *Clown* by Quentin Blake (1995) and *Up and Up* by Shirley Hughes (1979) in which there are no words and the story is told through pictures. The text is not there to connect the plot and describe the characters. The reader's response is what links picture to picture. The important element in these stories is that the reader has to work that little bit harder in order to understand the story.

Given that the illustrations play a crucial part in our understanding of many of the children's books we use, the following section enables us to reflect on some of the points made about the text in relation to the illustrations.

LOOKING AT THE PARTS

As with the written text, our response to the illustrations is affected by the various parts of a picture.

In the above example from Hoban and Blake's *How Tom Beat Captain Najork and his Hired Sportsmen* (1974), the illustration gives us some insight into how Aunt Fidget Wonkham-Strong feels about the Captain. It is a small part of the illustration but, as Tom suggests to the Captain the idea that she fancies him, Blake has put a wonderful expression on her face that says it all! This detail adds a lot to this part of the story.

One way of focusing attention on the smaller sections of illustrations is to cut two pieces of card into L-shapes. These are then placed over the illustration and turned to form a rectangle. The two parts of the rectangle can then be closed in or opened out to give a large or small frame.

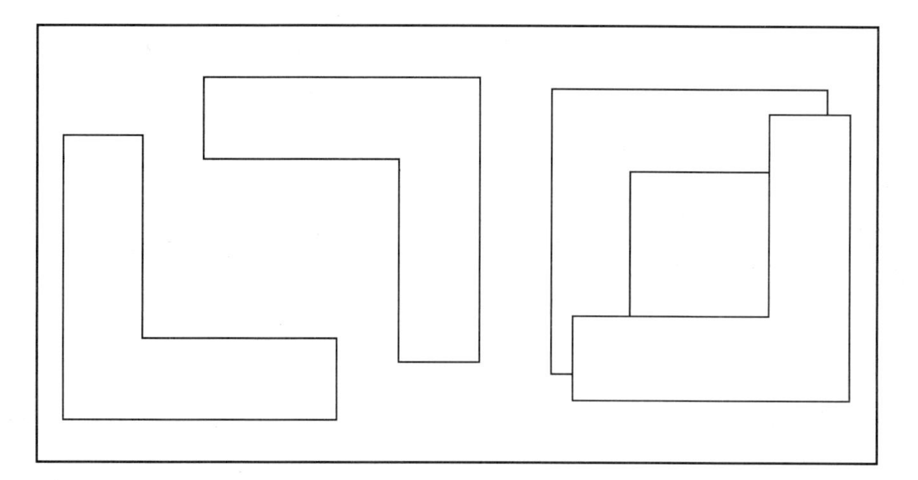

Children can then manipulate the L-shapes to close in on a part of the illustration. It may be the part they liked best of all or a particularly gory detail. There are often many parts of the complete illustration on which they focus, such as a face they thought looked particularly scary or a point where the main action is taking place on the page.

MODELS OF UNITY

As with text, we work to integrate the illustrations into our overall interpretation. This can work in two ways. The illustration can be present simply to complement our reading of the text. For example, in the Oxford Reading Tree book *Floppy's Bath* by Roderick Hunt (1989) the sentences are carefully structured to give the reader maximum support from the illustration: 'Floppy saw a rabbit' is complemented by a clear picture of the familiar character, Floppy, looking straight at the rabbit. If the words were missing, the reader would probably come up with a similar description of the event.

However, rather than illustrations confirming our reading of the text, they can also add to it. The wild things in Sendak's book *Where the Wild Things Are* are made all the more dramatic by the way they are depicted. Alternatively, illustrations can contrast with the text, as in a book like *Time to Get Out of the Bath, Shirley* by John Burningham (1978), in which Mum's

mundane prompting of Shirley to get a move on and get out of the bath is complemented by Shirley's trip down the plughole and into a fantasy land. When working on these types of book, it can sometimes be interesting to read the text before showing children the illustrations, as new paths of meaning will be provided when they are re-read showing the full pictures.

OPEN AND CLOSED

Some of the illustrations we encounter in stories deserve to be paused over. In Ian Beck's *Tom and the Island of Dinosaurs* there is a picture which shows the volcano erupting in a burst of colour across a double-page spread, and we also see the balloon that provides Tom's escape to one side of the erupting volcano. It is a simple enough part of the story but the illustration will often cause children to pause in order to understand it more fully. For younger children, time taken over a picture can prepare the ground for pausing over and being receptive to all they encounter as they mature in their reading of more open pieces of text.

F. THE TEXT: BLANKS AND GAPS

If we return briefly to the work of Wolfgang Iser, you will recall his image of the gap between two people in conversation being something like the gap between the text and the reader. The reader is involved in the task of filling the gaps or blanks, the indeterminacies. This involves using what is known to fill in what is not known. In this respect, the role of the reader involves a creative act of using what the text says to grasp that which is not said. From what is explicit the reader gathers what is implicit. Iser talks of the reader 'filling the blanks with projections'. The communication process that takes place involves an:

> interaction between the explicit and the implicit, between revelation and concealment. What is concealed spurs the reader into action... (page 111)

So the ending of Paul Jenning's story *Spaghetti Pig Out* (1988) is explicit. The reader is explicitly told that the hero has a magical video remote control that he can use on living things. He can pause them and fast-forward them. We are also told that the school bully, Guts, steals it and has his sidekick use it to fast-forward him in the school spaghetti-eating race so that he downs platefuls of spaghetti faster than anyone else. But we are also explicitly told that when Guts vomits an avalanche back up there is havoc. The hero grabs back the remote control and the last explicit part of this debacle states: 'I pointed the control at Guts and the river of sick. Then I pressed REWIND.' That's it. That's the end of explicit. What happens next is implicit. The reader does the rest. What is concealed spurs readers into action, filling the gaps with a projection!

This is the process the National Curriculum refers to when it states that children at Key Stage 2 *'should be taught inference and deduction'*. Doing this effectively involves making the most of texts like the ones above and their use of inference.

However, a word of caution. This should be done with care. Sometimes a blank that is explored is spoiled. Nothing spoils a joke more than having to dissect it painstakingly until the hearer 'gets' it. The blanks in a text work by being blanks.

I once finished reading *Spaghetti Pig Out* to a class just as the school day ended. I closed the book and said, 'Hometime!' The filling of the blank happened as the children made their way out of the door to groans of, 'Yuckk!' and, 'Oh, that's disgusting!' I didn't have to explain it. I let the gap in the text do its job.

In its references to inference, the Language programme of study is pointing out the need to make children aware of it and skilled in it. This can be done by focusing on the basic process of making and matching inferences.

MAKING INFERENCES

During the whole-class reading of texts, children will encounter some clear examples of gaps in the narrative that encourage creative filling in on their part. At the close of *Where the Wild*

Things Are, a reader could infer that there has been some move by Max's mother towards reconciliation. She remains unseen. She doesn't say anything to this effect. But Max returns to his room to find his supper waiting for him, still hot. That is the basis on which the reader can make an inference about the reconciliation.

In a sense the whole act of reading involves the reader in the process of making inferences. The two activities outlined below can also help children to recognise how people make inferences.

RUMMAGING

Objects collected and placed into a bin bag can provide clues about the activities of the bin's owner. Children can figure out what sorts of things they can infer from the evidence. For example, items such as an empty yoghurt pot, a cinema ticket, a bus ticket, a note saying 'Meet at 7.00pm' and a sketch map of the way to the town hall could enable the children to surmise facts such as 'He ate the yoghurt, caught the bus to the town hall and at 7.00pm met someone with whom he went to the cinema'.

This activity works especially well if a few groups have different bin bags containing various contents (the more items you put in the bag the more they will have to piece together!) and then come together to present their own evidence and deductions. If you construct a short story of your own similar to the one above as you choose items for the bags, it can be interesting to see how close a group can get to your scenario.

BEHIND THE PICTURE

Pictures can provide an excellent resource for making inferences. Photographs from advertisements or prints of works of art often contain indicators of a story, and local art galleries can provide a fascinating storehouse of stimuli for this activity. This involves looking at a painting and interpreting the action, working out how different characters are responding to each other and devising a story to link with the scene.

I remember taking a first school class around the Tate Gallery. We came across *Love and the Pilgrim* by Burne-Jones, a painting of an angelic figure taking a sad, hooded man by the hand, leading him out of thorns. In that silent gallery Gavin piped up with, 'Oi, Mr Thomas! Why is that fella pulling that girl into the bushes then?'

MATCHING

As reading of a text progresses, the reader's understanding of it is confirmed or altered. It is often worth keeping track of some of the inferences you make and seeing how they alter as the text progresses.

The way in which our inference is confirmed or contradicted by our reading is a major part of our comprehension of a story. Tony Ross's *I'm Coming to Get You* plays on this facet of reading, building up the expectation of the big monster confronting the little child, only to dash it when the final scene illustrates the shoe-sized monster. An awareness of the inferences the reader makes needs to be complemented by a matching of those inferences to the outcome we encounter in our reading.

STARS AND LINES: LOOKING AT WHO READERS ARE

We have already looked at Iser's image of the literary work taking place between two poles. The text is the artistic pole. The reader's realisation of the text is the aesthetic pole. One highly significant factor in the process of making sense of a text is the variety of responses that result from different readers interpreting the same text. This understanding of the role of the reader explains how the text will make sense in different ways to different readers, without there being one finalised meaning. This throws a new light on the responses children make to texts, the sharing of those responses with others and the place such responses take among the stock of reading experience they amass. If the meaning of the text arises as the reader responds to it then there are as many possible meanings as there are responses. There are as many responses as there are readers!

Looking at the aesthetic pole will involve the reader in reflecting on the role he or she plays in the making of meaning. This examination of the reader's role will be underscored by the objectives that he or she should:

✧ relate a text to his or her own experience, recognising the new experience offered in the act of reading;

✧ participate in activities that involve the sharing of responses to a story;

✧ relate a story to other stories he or she has read.

The main focus of this section is the individual reader and the understanding of the unique role he or she plays in the reading of literature.

STARGAZING: LOOKING AT THE READER

Two readers will differ in their reading of a text because *they* are different. Reader response theory examines and works with readers' varied responses to texts. For the teacher it involves valuing children's responses as a unique making of meaning. As Iser (in Freund) says:

> ...two people gazing at the night sky may both be looking at the same collection of stars, but one will see the image of a plough, and the other will make out a dipper. The 'stars' in a literary text are fixed; the lines that join them are variable. (page 146)

Acknowledging this will involve resisting a temptation to 'hammer home' one interpretation of the meaning of a story. Such a thing as a single 'true' interpretation does not exist! It will instead involve focusing on trying to work with whatever responses arise from individuals' encounter with the text. Such individuality will be seen in the different ways children relate to a text, are extended by a text and analyse their responses to a text, both on their first encounter and on revisiting the story.

A. LOOKING AT THE READER: RELATING

I recently read *Pandora's Box* to a class of children who were quite taken with the idea of flouting a serious prohibition (in this case 'Don't open the box'). It only took one member of the class to say that his mum had a similar prohibition about playing by the main road and... whoosshhh! – a forest of arms went up, each with a prohibition to relate. This is an experience that I am sure is common to many readers of this book, the unprompted discussion that 'takes off' and then takes a while to come down again!

Our understanding of reader response theory may alter our view of this type of occurrence. The things we may be tempted to dismiss as interruptions take on a new significance when we recognise the important link they offer between the text and the individual. Relating text to personal experience brings alive the words on the page. Of course, teachers need to balance encouragement and discussion of such responses with a need to keep to a timetable but equally, when planning that timetable, it is important to bear in mind the value attached to such 'interruptions'. They should be expected, acknowledged and encouraged.

We also need to ensure that the full breadth of responses is acknowledged. One of my class recently ended our reading of the story of *Orpheus* with the response, 'He was a bit thick to look back!' Well – that is her response! I could offer my response, but she was resolute. He was thick!

Relating story to experience involves engaging with the emotional impact of the story. There are often situations in which literature has a unique resonance with a reader. Helen Cresswell (in R. Lewis, 1975) sees an exciting potential for reading to ring true with experience as a reader encounters a text in which:

> the reader is experiencing things which perhaps he... never had words for and this gives meaning for this feeling, because there it is in words... it actually exists. (page 175)

As the child encounters the text, there will be those responses that arise from a resonance. The text rings true with his or her own experience. A book like Sheldon and Blythe's *The Whales' Song* gives some expression to that childhood longing to see something magical. Books that depict experiences of racism, such as Mary Hoffman and Caroline Binch's *Amazing Grace* (1991), or parent problems, such as Philip Ridley's *Meteorite Spoon* (1994), provide the possibility of an expression to which a child can relate. This may be a private response and, as teachers, we need to be sensitive to that. In whatever context it occurs, there is a unique act of the making of meaning to be encouraged whenever a child feels moved to say or to imply 'I recognise what this story is saying. In some way it happened to me'.

B. LOOKING AT THE READER: EXTENDING

Following on from the potential for this resonance with the reader, there is also a potential for stories to alter us. They take personal experience and extend it. In his book *The Dark Interval* (1975) Crossan shows this process of working on the reader to be crucial to the actions of parables. They criss-cross expectations. The wounded man lies at the roadside. The listeners expect the priest and the Levite will do the right thing and help him out. They also assume that Samaritans cannot be trusted. So the expectation is that the clergy will help and the Samaritan is a rat. The twist in the tale is that the Samaritan helps and the injured man's kin and clergy are the rats. The parable shocks and alters its listeners. A new light is cast on the debate about who helps whom and the audience have their horizons widened.

Stories can also extend personal experience by taking their readers to a place where they have not been before. In *Where the Wild Things Are*, as the white frame around the illustrations becomes smaller and smaller and the pictures take over the page there is a sense in which the reader is being drawn into this land and its 'wild rumpus'. In working with children on their responses to stories we can open up the idea of stories taking us beyond the norm. This will involve looking at the new experiences stories offer their readers and drawing upon children's expressions of, for example, what it was like to face the dilemma of finding hundreds of pounds. This experiential aspect of reading is expressed admirably by C.S. Lewis (1961):

> We want to see with other eyes, to imagine with other imaginations, to feel with other hearts, as well as with our own. (page 137)

C. LOOKING AT THE READER: ANALYSING

Meaning is a creative act. To use Iser's image, the stars are fixed but the lines are creatively perceived. Reading with an emphasis on the role of the reader's response will fuel a teacher's desire to involve readers in analysing their responses. What we want to avoid is the 'hole in my bucket' cycle, as Fenwick (1990) calls it, which runs:

> 'Why do you like this book?'
> 'Because it is nice.'
> 'Why is it nice?'
> 'Because I like it.'
> 'Why do you like this book?'... (page 53)

Children need to be given a structure to prompt a more constructive analysis of their response. Underpinning most of these ideas is the need to move beyond, 'Why do you like this book?' to something more tangible for a child. Having established a child's initial response to a book, we need more focused questions such as:

- Find me your favourite page.
- What did you think was the funniest part?
- Who was your favourite character?
- Who was your second favourite?
- What did you think was good about the ending?

- ✧ What would have made this story better?
- ✧ What did it remind you of?

Specific analysis breaks the 'hole in my bucket' cycle.

D. LOOKING AT THE READER: REVISITING

Children's stories, like many other creative works, merit a second visit. Most teachers at Key Stage 1 will know only too well the experience of children selecting the same book day after day for storytime. Revisiting is important because our creative act of making sense of a text can alter each time we return to it. Reading with foresight has a pleasure all of its own. Clues are heard, nuances noticed that were missed first time around. For example, on re-reading Roderick Hunt's *What a Bad Dog* (1989) children often notice Dad leaving the tray on the cooker where it will cause a fire. In *The Chase* (1989), also by Hunt, they notice, second time around, that Floppy is not tied properly to the lamppost.

Revisiting a text some years after a first reading can also provide an interesting focus for analysing and comparing responses. Asking children at Key Stage 2 to look at some of their earliest books can provide some nostalgic reflection.

COMMUNITY OF RESPONSE

'Ah!' you will say, 'if the reader is the one who creates the meaning of the text, what is to stop me reading this paragraph and deciding that what you have written is actually a recipe for mushroom soup?' To which I would reply with two points. First, the fact is that if you wanted to read that into my writing I am not there to stop you. The author is absent. I've gone. But my guess is that because of the fixed nature of some of the parts of this text, like the stars in the sky in Iser's analogy, you won't do that. Secondly, our readings are influenced, if not governed, by our experience in the community within which we read. Stanley Fish (1976) sees the community within which we respond to be the answer to the conundrum, 'Why should two or more readers ever agree...?' (page 169).

> Why, if meaning is created by the individual reader from the perspective of his own experience and interpretive desires, is there so much that interpreters agree about? (1989, page 141)

For Fish the answer lies in the authority that arises from the interpretive community.

> Interpretive communities are made up of those who share interpretive strategies... these strategies exist prior to the act of reading and therefore determine the shape of what is read... (1976, page 169)

Another seam of working with stories is opened by this insight. We can work with children exploring their responses as part of an interpretive community.

A. THE COMMUNITY: IDENTIFYING

A significant part of children's reflection on themselves as responding readers can be made up of looking back at the interaction that made them readers. Roald Dahl (1977) provides some insight into his own initiation into the literacy club. The cruel regime at his boarding school was broken each Saturday morning when the masters went to the pub and the children were all left with 'Blessed beautiful Mrs O'Connor':

> But Mrs O'Connor was no baby-sitter. She was nothing less than a great and gifted teacher...
>
> She had the great teacher's knack of making everything she spoke about come alive to us in that room. In two and a half hours, we grew to love Langland and his Piers Plowman. (pages 198–199)

Children can look at the process by which they became readers and the influences others had on the process. As they do this they will often focus on things that made reading work well then, such as a supportive adult or a desire to find out what happened at the end of a story. Elaine Millard (1994) has worked with children on their stories of how they learned to read, presenting the story of their reading development in a variety of literary forms. Such reflections latch on to the range of books the child has worked with and the various adults who encouraged this development.

B. THE COMMUNITY: PARTICIPATING

The primary school is a place where the community of readers takes on a tangible form. The texts we work with are often designed for interaction. Songs like *Football Crazy* and *The Bear in the Woods* are stories put up on overhead projectors and sung together. Many of the picture books we read involve us talking a whole class through a story, often with a high level of interaction. Group reading involves children sitting in a circle, focusing on the same story. Texts that encourage the participation of a whole group provide a way of working directly with a whole class's interaction with the text.

Big books are an excellent means of sharing with a whole class in the reading of a story. The work of the National Literacy Project has revived the use of such formats. The large print allows the teacher to model the process of reading through the words on the page, raising questions and issues encountered along the way and guiding the children through the reading. The sorts of responses looked at in this chapter can be worked through as the whole group interacts with the story.

While there are a number of manufactured big books now available, there is still a lot to be said for using school-made copies. The farm trip or the visit of a theatre group, some of the run-of-the mill activities in which we participate – these can provide the raw material for stories, and children will often warm to the task of illustrating appropriate pages.

C. THE COMMUNITY: SHARING

Our consideration of the community that develops and guides a child's responses highlights the importance of sharing responses.

One of the most entertaining elements of being a reader can be the discussion with fellow readers of the texts we share in common. Working with another person is, for all of us, a critical means of eliciting the fullest response we can give to literature.

This raises the need both to stimulate and to structure a process. Just sending a couple of six-year-old children off into a corner to share their responses to a particular story won't work. Something more is needed to structure the task. One way of doing this is to ask children to share the part they liked the most with a partner. They can then swap partners with another partnership and share again. Then swap and share again. At this point it can be worthwhile stopping the group to see if one part of the story is emerging as a common favourite. One or two individuals can be asked to recall, not their own responses, but the responses they have heard so far.

One of the most useful ways of structuring this process is the 'Tell me' approach of Aiden Chambers, described in *Tell Me: Children, Reading and Talk* (1993).

'TELL ME...'

Chambers describes his approach as 'a way of asking particular kinds of question'. Chambers worked with teachers in drawing out children's responses to texts. They banned the question 'Why?' as in 'Why did you like this book?' and instead started with four basic booktalk questions:

> 'Tell me...
> – Was there anything that you liked about this book?
> – Was there anything that you disliked?
> – Was there anything that puzzled you?
> – Were there any patterns – any connections – that you noticed?' (page 76)

Responses to these questions are then listed in parallel columns. Once the four lists are compiled, the children look for topics that are shown in more than one column and link them together. The links that form, showing the prevalence of one or two issues or themes, are highlighted as topics for further discussion. The topic that has the most connections is used as a starting point.

INTERTEXTUALITY

> *I read the text...* This 'I' which approaches the text is already itself a plurality of other texts... (in Barthes, 1990, page 10)

Intertextuality is the relationship readers create between a text they read and the other texts they have experienced. This can involve a number of links being made between the text being read and other texts – such as seeing similarities and making comparisons. Barthes, in the quotation above, is referring to the library of texts that have contributed to the experience of the reader. Readers constantly cross-refer to other reading experiences. Indeed, our acquisition of reading has depended on us strengthening our ability with certain texts and then applying this ability to other texts. In the classroom we can work with these intertextual links in the following ways.

INTERTEXTUALITY: LINKING TEXTS

Primary teachers are already used to linking texts. The use of projects to give some structure to medium-term planning often leads to the reading of books that share a common connection with the project theme. If the project is 'Dinosaurs', for example, one of the books chosen may be Beck's *Tom and the Island of Dinosaurs* (1995).

We need to ensure that such links make the most of all that literature can offer. Superficially, there will be some obvious links between titles and projects. Examining more closely what a reader could gather from a book will sometimes expose deeper links between texts. For example, how many story books deal with the broader themes of 'the past'? These themes may complement a study of the chosen topic.

To give a clear example, there are a number of books that use dinosaurs. They are excellent titles. But there are also excellent books about the way in which pieces of the past impinge on the present with an alluring fascination. Books such as *The Garden* by Dyan Sheldon and Gary Blythe and *All the Kings and Queens* by Jan Mark (1993) deal with other historical periods affecting the present day. Could it be that as well as looking at texts that have the superficial link of the main subject of the topic we can also look at texts to explore some of the deeper significance of topics? There is still a place for those clear-cut topic links that involve collecting together and reading books on the topic itself. However, what can also be drawn out of a topic are some of the deeper themes that link it to a range of stories.

To illustrate how the links between texts can operate on the deeper level of the underlying theme rather than the superficial level of the subject matter, look at the list of suggested themes below. They may not be typical but may still suggest certain stories that would fit the topic:

✧ wanting – the idea of a deep longing for something or someone;

✧ being in trouble – the exploration of the feelings and actions we take when we are in trouble;

✧ doorways – stories that deal with doorways or ways of reaching into other worlds.

Here are some examples of stories I could find:

✧ wanting – Grace's longing to take part in the school play in Hoffman and Binch's *Amazing Grace*; Jenny's longing for something more to life in Sendak's *Higglety, Pigglety, Pop*; and Lily's longing to see the whales in Sheldon and Blythe's *The Whales' Song*;

✧ being in trouble – the narrative poem 'Babysitter' in Michael Rosen's *The Hypnotiser* (1988); Ba getting into trouble in Millar's *On Your Potty*; and the two children on the run in Thomas's *The Runaways* (1987).

✧ doorways – a plughole in John Burningham's *Time to Get Out of the Bath, Shirley*; a wardrobe in C.S. Lewis's *The Lion, the Witch and the Wardrobe*; and a book in Ende's *The Neverending Story*.

INTERTEXTUALITY: COMPARING TEXTS

Once children start to link texts they also start to compare texts. They evaluate them by holding one against another. These comparisons involve an essential element of personal response. The task of building such comparisons into our teaching can be structured in a number of ways:

COMPARING TWO STORIES ON THE SAME SUBJECT

In Robert Munsch's *The Paper Bag Princess* and Martin Waddell's *The Tough Princess*, the princesses both undertake a quest to get their prince. One ends up rejecting hers, the other biffs him then marries him. There is an obvious similarity but our happiness with the ending of each tale gives some insight into our response to the two different princesses and their potential suitors. Similarly, Betsy Byars' *The Eighteenth Emergency* (1973) deals with bullying in a very different way to Alan Gibbons' *Chicken* (1993). Both books are similar in a number of ways, making the differences (for example, the use of humour in Byars' title) all the more interesting. In both the above examples the similarities enhance the distinctiveness of each story.

PARODY

Parody is a literary method that makes the fullest use of such comparisons. The charm of *The Paper Bag Princess* lies in the way it is similar to so many conventional fairy tales. This makes the differences all the more entertaining. Stories such as Jon Scieszka's parodies in *The Stinky Cheese Man and other Fairly Stupid Tales* (1993) introduce the youngest readers to this device as Scieszka's ugly duckling grows up into an ugly duck. From a young age children will enjoy seeing the story forms they become used to being parodied in this way.

As children begin to understand how such parodies work, there appears an obvious gateway into writing activities. They will be able to explore a literary style by parodying it themselves. The production of fairy tales in which the villain wins is the sort of activity that engages with the concept of parody and explores the make up of that which is parodied.

KEEPING RESPONSES

Fish (1980) likened reading experience to the creativity of a dancer. This being so, as children work their way through school it is important to keep a selection of responses to show their development in this creative skill. Keeping such records of response can also provide an assessment tool for the teacher. I would like to close this chapter with three practical ways of turning readings into writing that gives concrete expression to the response of the reader.

READING LOGS

A number of schools now maintain a record system in which children record their responses to the books they read. The brevity of comment required lessens the sense that this is a chore. The most effective records of this nature I have seen in use are those that remain with the reader throughout his or her time at school, building up a long-term record.

If such records are to be put in place, children need some guidance as to what they should write in the section headed 'Comment'. The sorts of activities described throughout this book should provide the basis for possible comments. For example, they may wish to base their comment on something about the language that is used to describe a villain, or they may prefer to record their feelings towards the suspense in a story.

WRITING FRAMES

One of the most useful tools for developing a range of writing is the writing frame, in which a framework for a piece of writing is provided using certain phrases that guide its form. The book *Developing Children's Non-fiction Writing: Working with Writing Frames* by Lewis and Wray (1995) shows how these can develop various forms of writing including the persuasive and the explanatory.

The frame consists of words and phrases that give a lead-in to a piece of writing by providing a structure. For example, an explanation frame opens with the sentence starter, 'I would like to persuade you that...' This is followed by the next sentence starter, 'There are several reasons for this. The chief reason is...' A set of such starters provides the child with a frame to use in writing an explanation.

Looking back at the material covered in this book should provide the material for a number of new writing frames that would structure a child's response to a story. The writing below shows Alameh's response to the myth of Perseus. She was given a variety of sentence starters from which to construct her own piece of writing. These were 'I thought...', 'I liked...', 'I didn't like...', 'I was puzzled...' and 'It reminded me...' This gave her the format to make a written response to the story.

I thougt perseus would die.
I Liked the bit when perseus chaps of medusas hed of.
I dident Like when the King turens in to Stone.
I was puzzled when Perseus became a King.
It reminded me of my dad allways worried about something.
I Like when the King says to dance to marrie him and she say's no.

A frame is an adaptable idea. The sorts of frame we could set include ones with a focus on the events in the storyline:

> At the start...
> At the end...
> The difference between the start and the end was...
> The difference was caused by...

Or on the characters:

> The character I like the most is...
> I like the character because...
> I know this about them because...
> This character reminded me of...

Taking the elements of poetics looked at in the preceding chapters and turning them into frames would provide the potential for a rich record of response.

WRITING FROM A TEXT

Creative writing stimulated by a text is not a new idea. For example, children may be asked to listen *to The Frog Prince* and to write a story about the prince's life as a frog, or to read McKee's *Not Now, Bernard* and write an alternative ending. However, the depth of the story can provide material for such activities (see 'Linking texts', page 172). A story such as *The Frog Prince* could stimulate writing based on:

- ✧ feeling ugly;
- ✧ being rejected;
- ✧ being found by someone;
- ✧ losing a precious possession;
- ✧ someone changing.

There is a depth to many of these stories that can be linked with other similar tales. The result can be a foundation in literary exploration of a theme that can stimulate further writing.

CONCLUSION

Writers such as Iser and Fish bring the process of reading and the making of meaning alive in vivid ways. They point us towards a process we may have taken for granted and show just how much there is to it, so much of which readers slip into as second nature. Reflecting upon how children make meaning as they read can develop our own understanding of the creative process of reading, and enable us to guide children in ways which will enable them to grow in their understanding of the experience of reading and to learn more about the process of responding.

AFTERWORD

The conclusion to this book lies in the classroom, where the suggestions and ideas in it can be tried and tested. So this afterword offers some starters to complement the use of the theoretical and practical material in this book so far. By now, anyone reading this book will have a range of strategies for working with texts. In the following section I present four issues that underpin such work.

READ STORIES TO THE CLASS

It is surprising the extent to which the practice of reading stories has slipped out of the classroom routine. The recent strictures on the number of hours that must be allocated to specific subjects have, in some cases, had a detrimental effect on this crucial part of the school's role in introducing children to stories. This is not to belittle some of the recent strides that have been made in the teaching of literacy. Instead it is a recognition of the need, within planning for literacy, to build up a child's experience of story. To this end, nothing will replace the experience of a good story being read well to a class of enthralled children.

As far as the 'good' story part of this requirement is concerned, it may be worth using some of the theory in this book as a means of assessing the quality of literature being used. I am loath to pronounce some criteria for assessing the difference between a 'good' and a 'not good' story. However, I would suggest that it is worth seeking out those stories that engage a reader with some of those aspects of the poetics of story covered in this book. The way in which a plot works out in a story, the nature of the characterisation, the way in which the response of the reader is drawn out – for me as a teacher, these are the sorts of things that make for a quality story. This suggestion draws on C.S. Lewis's idea (1961) of 'defining good literature as that which permits, invites or even compels good reading' (page 104).

PLAN FOR THE TEACHING OF STORY

If nothing else, it is to be hoped that this book has demonstrated the complexities that can be identified and examined when looking at the poetic aspects of a story. These aspects are set down in the national curricula. They are also prominent in the guidelines of the National Literacy Project. Above all, they stand out in stories as important parts of the stories themselves.

As schools turn to the task of using national guidelines to feed into their English policies and schemes of work, it is worth planning in the teaching of the varied aspects of literacy covered in this book. For example, making a clear commitment to teaching the meaning of the term 'character' in the early years can be followed up by a commitment to develop a child's awareness of the roles characters play at a later stage. This is a working book. It suggests that such awareness needs to be taught and offers some ways of teaching it. The next question for the school is 'Who will teach it – and when?'

GENERATE AN ENTHUSIASM FOR LITERACY

In my experience, one of the single most powerful tools for developing the commitment of a group of children to the exploration of stories has been their encounter with a group of staff who generate enthusiasm around the subject. Teachers who read and share stories they are excited about using in the classroom can impart to children an infectious love of stories.

To this end the enthusiast needs to be an ambassador for story. This may involve finding out what topics are being covered in various classes and suggesting the story that would make an effective input or scribbling out a set of suggestions for working with such a story. In some ways this ventures on to the role of the English co-ordinator. So many of the activities that build up the school's enthusiasm in this area, such as book weeks and the building up of the school library, usually fall to the co-ordinator. However, the sort of collective enthusiasm I am describing cannot be a one-woman or one-man show. It stems from colleagues collaborating in the task of reading, sharing and suggesting good stories to one another and to the children.

CONCLUSION

The past 15 years have seen significant debate over the teaching of reading. The term 'real book' gained much currency, describing the sort of book that was not constricted by the set vocabulary of a particular scheme. This approach was caricatured in the media as a band of whacky teachers slinging out all the phonics and the reading books. In fact, the practice of using 'real books' and promoting 'real reading' denoted the belief that 'enjoyment brings achievement more powerfully than structure, sequence, staged materials' (Allen, 1989).

In reality, very few teachers completely discarded all grasp of sequence or structure. What writers such as Meek and Waterland brought to our practice was a sense of the importance of the enjoyment children gain from the meaning of the text and a demonstration of how important it was in fostering the skills of reading.

What makes many of us readers is our involvement in the things we read. We are gripped, entertained, amused and shocked by what we read – so we read more. This book has presented the sort of engagement with texts that can still work with the structure and staging of planned literacy teaching. But it makes a plea that as we continue to promote literacy we should aim for a literacy that is meaningful. We have to avoid teaching a reading that makes the right noises when it sees the right words. Creative literacy, *real* literacy – literacy that leads to readers who will keep on reading and use those skills to their full – is something that comes from the response of the reader. The theorists we have encountered speak of reading being like stargazing and dancing. These are images that sound more like the experience we have when we're *really* reading.

BIBLIOGRAPHY

*Ahlberg, J. and A. (1978) *Each Peach Pear Plum*, Viking Kestrel.

Allen, D. (1989) 'What's Real about "Real Reading"' in *Building a House of Fiction*, NATE.

Bal, M. (1985) *Narratology: Introduction to the Theory of Narrative*, Toronto.

Barthes, R. (1977) 'Introduction to the Structural Analysis of Narratives' in *Image–Music–Text*, Fontana (original publication in French, 1966).

Barthes, R. (1990) *S/Z*, Blackwell (original publication in French, 1973).

*Beck, I. (1995) *Tom and the Island of Dinosaurs*, Picture Corgi.

Berlin, A. (1983) *Poetics and Interpretation of Biblical Narrative*, Almond Press.

*Blake, Q. (1995) *Clown*, Jonathan Cape.

Booth, W.C. (1961) *The Rhetoric of Fiction*, University of Chicago Press.

Bremond, C. (1980) 'The Logic of Narrative Possibilities' in Onega and Garcia Landa (original publication in French, 1966).

Brogan, H. (1990) *The Penguin History of the United States of America*, Penguin.

*Brown, R. (1981) *A Dark, Dark Tale*, Andersen Press.

*Browne, A. (1989) *The Tunnel*, Julia MacRae.

*Browne, A. (1976) *Through the Magic Mirror*, Hamish Hamilton Ltd.

*Browne, A. (1984) *Willy the Wimp*, Julia MacRae.

*Burnett, F. Hodgson (1905) *A Little Princess*.

*Burnett, F. Hodgson (1911) *The Secret Garden*.

*Burningham, J. (1978) *Time to Get Out of the Bath, Shirley*, Jonathan Cape.

*Byars, B. (1973) *The Eighteenth Emergency*, Bodley Head.

Cairney, T.H. (1995) *Pathways to Literacy*, Cassell.

Calvino, I. (1981) *If on a Winter's Night a Traveller*, Secker and Warburg (original publication in Italian, 1979).

*Cave, K. (1994) *Something Else*, Viking.

Chambers, A. (1993) *Tell Me: Children, Reading and Talk*, Thimble Press.

*Chapman, H. (1996) *The Treasure of the Stone Lions*, Heinemann.

Chatman, S. (1978) *Story and Discourse: Narrative Structure in Fiction and Film*, Cornell.

Cohan, S. and Shires, L. (1988) *Telling Stories: A Theoretical Analysis of Fiction*, Routledge.

Cox, B. (1989) *English for Ages 5 to 16* ('The Cox Report'), National Curriculum Council.

*Cresswell, H. (1993) *The Watchers*, Viking.

Crossan, J.D. (1975) *The Dark Interval: Towards a Theology of Story*, Argus Communications.

Culler, J. (1975) *Structuralist Poetics: Structuralism, Linguistics and the Study of Literature*, Routledge.

Culler, J. (1981) *The Pursuit of Signs: Semiotics, Literature, Deconstruction*, Routledge and Kegan Paul.

*Dahl, R. (1984) *Boy: Tales of Childhood*, Jonathan Cape.

*Dahl, R. (1967) *Charlie and the Chocolate Factory*, Jonathan Cape.

*Dahl, R. (1975) *Danny the Champion of the World*, Puffin.

*Dahl, R. (1981) *George's Marvellous Medicine*, Jonathan Cape.

*Dahl, R. (1967) *James and the Giant Peach*, Allen & Unwin.

*Dahl, R. (1988) *Matilda*, Jonathan Cape.

*Dahl, R. (1983) *The Sheep-Pig*, Puffin.

*Dahl, R. (1983) *The Witches*, Puffin

*Dahl, R. (1977) *The Wonderful Story of Henry Sugar*, Jonathan Cape.

DFE (1995) *Key Stages 1 and 2 of the National Curriculum*, HMSO.

Dubrow, H. (1988) *Genre*, Methuen.

Eco, U. (1979) *The Role of the Reader: Explorations in the Semiotics of Texts*, Hutchinson.

*Ende, M. (1983) *The Neverending Story*, Doubleday (original publication in German, 1979).

Fenwick, G. (1990) *Teaching Children's Literature in the Primary School*, David Fulton.

*Fine, A. (1996) *How to Write Really Badly*, Methuen.

Fish, S. (1989) *Doing What Comes Naturally: Change, Rhetoric and the Practice of Theory in Literary and Legal Studies*, Clarendon Press.

Fish, S. (1976) 'Interpreting the Variorum' in Rylance (ed.) (1987).

Fish, S. (1970) 'Literature in the Reader: Affective Stylistics' in Tomkins (1980).

*Fisher, C. (1993) *The Snow Walker's Son*, Bodley Head.

Forster, E.M. (1927) *Aspects of the Novel*, Penguin.

*Forward, T. (1992) *Wivern Winter*, Andersen Press.

Freund, E. (1987) *The Return of the Reader: Reader Response Criticism*, Methuen.

*Garfield, L. (1984) 'The Lamplighter's Funeral' in *Six Apprentices*, Heinemann.

Genette, G. (1980) *Narrative Discourse: An Essay in Method*, Cornell (original publication in French, 1972).

*Gibbons, A. (1993) *Chicken*, Dent.

*Gibson, A. (1989) *Ellis and the Hummick*, Faber.

Green, K. and LeBihan, J. (1996) *Critical Theory and Practice: A Coursebook*, Routledge.

Greimas, A.J. (1983) *Structural Semantics: An Attempt at Method*, University of Nebraska Press (original publication in French, 1966).

Hawkes, T. (1977) *Structuralism and Semiotics*, Routledge.

*Heide, F. Parry (1971) *The Shrinking of Treehorn*, Puffin.

*Hendry, D. (1991) *Harvey Angell*, Julia MacRae.

Hendy, L. (1994) 'From Drama into Story: Strategies for Investigating Texts' in Styles, Bearne and Watson.

*Hoban, R. (1986) *The Marzipan Pig*, Jonathan Cape.

*Hoban, R. and Blake, Q. (1974) *How Tom Beat Captain Najork and his Hired Sportsmen*, Jonathan Cape/Red Fox.

*Hoffman, M. and Binch, C. (1991) *Amazing Grace*, Frances Lincoln.

Holland, N. (1980) 'Unity Identity Text Self' in Tomkins (ed.) (1980).

*Howarth, L. (1994) *Maphead*, Walker.

*Hughes, S. (1981) *Alfie Gets in First*, Bodley Head.

*Hughes, S. (1983) *Alfie Gives a Hand*, Bodley Head.

*Hughes, S. (1977) *Dogger*, Bodley Head.

*Hughes, S. (1993) 'Sea Singing' in *Stories by Firelight*, Bodley Head.

*Hughes, S. (1979) *Up and Up*, Bodley Head.

*Hughes, T. (1968) *The Iron Man*, Faber.

Hunt, G. (1994) 'Meeting Morris Gleitzmann' in *Books for Keeps*, No. 84, School Bookshop Association.

Hunt, G. (1994) 'Philip Ridley' in *Books for Keeps*, No. 85, School Bookshop Association.

*Hunt, R. (1989) *The Chase* in Oxford Reading Tree series, Oxford University Press.

*Hunt, R. (1989) *Floppy's Bath* in Oxford Reading Tree series, Oxford University Press.

*Hunt, R. (1989) *What a Bad Dog* in Oxford Reading Tree series, Oxford University Press.

*Hutchins, P. (1968) *Rosie's Walk*, Bodley Head.

*Ibbotson, E. (1994) *The Secret of Platform 13*, Macmillan.

*Impey, R. (1992) 'Rumplestiltskin' in *The Orchard Book of Fairy Tales*, Orchard.

Iser, W. (1980) 'Interaction Between Text and Reader' in Suleiman, S.R. and Crosman, I.

*James, S. (1991) *Dear Greenpeace*, Walker.

*Jennings, P. (1994) *The Gizmo*, Penguin.

*Jennings, P. (1995) *The Gizmo Again*, Penguin.

*Jennings, P. (1987) 'The Busker' in *Unbelievable*, Penguin.

*Jennings, P. (1988) 'Spaghetti Pig Out' in *Uncanny*, Puffin.

*Jones, T. (1981) 'The Fly-by-Night' in *Fairy Tales*, Pavilion.

*Jones. T. (1985) *Nicobobinus*, Pavilion.

*King-Smith, D. (1992) *The Finger Eater*, Walker.

*King-Smith, D. (1983) *The Sheep-Pig*, Victor Gollancz Ltd.

Knowles, M. and Malmkjaer, K. (1996) *Language and Control in Children's Literature*, Routledge.

*Koralek, J. (1994) *The Boy and the Cloth of Dreams*, Walker.

Kuhn, T.S. (1970) *The Structure of Scientific Revolutions*, University of Chicago Press.

Lawson, M. (1995) *Idlewild or Everything is Subject to Change*, Picador.

*Leeson, R. (1975) *The Third Class Genie*, Lions.

Lewis, C.S. (1961) *An Experiment in Criticism*, Cambridge University Press.

*Lewis, C.S. (1950) *The Lion, the Witch and the Wardrobe*, Geoffrey Bles.

*Lewis, C.S. (1951) *Prince Caspian*, Geoffrey Bles.

Lewis, M. and Wray, D. (1995) *Developing Children's Non-fiction Writing: Working with Writing Frames*, Scholastic.

Lewis, R. (1975) 'Fiction and the Imagination' in *Children's Literature in Education*, No. 19, A.P.S. Publications Inc.

*Mark, J. (1993) *All the Kings and Queens*, Heinemann.

*Mark, J. (1992) *The Snow Maze*, Walker.

Marsh, J. (1996) 'The Play in the Picture Book' in *Language and Learning* (Oct/Nov), Questions Publishing.

Martin, T. and Leather, B. (1994) *Readers and Texts in the Primary Years*, Open University Press.

Martin, W. (1986) *Recent Theories of Narrative*, Cornell.

*McKee, D. (1980) *Not Now, Bernard*, Andersen Press.

*McKee, D. (1987) *Two Monsters*, Beaver Books.

Meek, M. (1988) *How Texts Teach What Readers Learn*, The Thimble Press.

Meek, Warlow and Barton (eds.) (1977) *The Cool Web: The Pattern of Children's Reading*, Bodley Head.

*Millar, V. (1991) *On Your Potty*, Walker.

Millard, E. (1994) *Developing Readers in the Middle Years*, Open University Press.

*Munsch, R. (1982) *The Paper Bag Princess*, Scholastic.

*Murphy, J. (1982) *On the Way Home*, Macmillan.

Naidoo, B. (1985) *Journey to Jo'burg: A South African Story*, Longman.

NLP (1997) *The National Literacy Project Framework for Teaching (Draft)*, National Literacy Project.

OFSTED (1996) *The Teaching of Reading in 45 Inner London Primary Schools*, OFSTED.

Onega, S. and Garcia Landa, J. (eds.) (1996) *Narratology*, Longman.

*Oxenbury, H. (1988) *Tom and Pippo and the Washing Machine*, Walker.

Powell, M.A. (1993) *What is Narrative Criticism: A New Approach to the Bible*, SPCK.

*Price, S. (1987) *The Ghost Drum*, Faber.

Propp, V. (1968) *The Morphology of the Folk Tale*, University of Texas (original publication in Russian, 1928).

*Ridley, P. (1989) *Dakota of the White Flats*, William Collins Sons & Co. Ltd.

*Ridley, P. (1994) *Kaspar and the Glitter*, Viking.

*Ridley, P. (1991) *Krindlekrax*, Jonathan Cape.

*Ridley, P. (1994) *Meteorite Spoon*, Viking.

Rimmon-Kenan, S. (1983) *Narrative Fiction: Contemporary Poetics*, Methuen.

*Rosen, M. (1987) *A Spider Bought a Bicycle and Other Poems*, Kingfisher.

*Rosen, M. (1988) *The Hypnotiser*, André Deutsch.

*Rosen, M. (1990) *Little Rabbit Foo Foo*, Walker.

*Rosen, M. (1983) 'Go-kart' in *Quick, Let's Get Out of Here*, André Deutsch.

*Rosen, M. (ed.) (1992) *South and North, East and West*, Walker.

*Rosen, M. (1989) *We're Going on a Bear Hunt*, Walker.

*Rosen, M. (1990) *The Wicked Tricks of Till Owlyglass*, Walker.

*Ross, T. (1984) *I'm Coming to Get You*, Andersen Press.

*Ross, T. (1987) *Oscar Got the Blame*, Andersen Press.

*Ross, T. (1988) *Super Dooper Jezebel*, Andersen Press.

*Russell, C. and Russell, C. (1989) *Through the Dragon's Eye*, BBC Books.

Rylance, R. (1987) *Debating Texts: A Reader in Twentieth-Century Literary Theory and Method*, Open University Press.

Saussure, F. de (1960) *Course in General Linguistics*, Peter Owen (original publication in French, 1915).

*Scieszka, J. (1993) *The Stinky Cheese Man and other Fairly Stupid Tales*, Puffin.

*Scott, H. (1989) *Freddie and the Enormouse*, Walker.

Selden, R. (1985) *A Reader's Guide to Contemporary Literary Theory*, Harvester.

Selden, R. (1989) *Practising Theory and Reading Literature: An Introduction*, Harvester Wheatsheaf.

*Sendak, M. (1967) *Higglety Pigglety Pop! or There Must Be More To Life*, Harper and Row.

*Sendak, M. (1967) *Where the Wild Things Are*, Bodley Head.

*Sheldon, D. and Blythe, G. (1993) *The Garden*, Hutchinson.

*Sheldon, D. and Blythe, G. (1990) *The Whales' Song*, Hutchinson.

Smith, F. (1985) *Reading* (second edition), Cambridge University Press.

SOED (1991) *English Language 5–14 National Guidelines*, HMSO.

Southgate, Arnold and Johnson (1981) *Extending Beginning Reading*, Schools Council/Heinemann.

*Spinelli, J. (1995) *Maniac Magee*, Scholastic.

*Stine, R.L. Goosebumps series, Scholastic.

*Storr, C. (1980) *Clever Polly and the Stupid Wolf*, Faber.

Styles, M., Bearne E. and Watson W. (eds.) (1994) *The Prose and the Passion*, Cassell.

Suleiman, S.R. and Crosman, I. (eds.) (1980) *The Reader in the Text: Essays on Audience and Interpretation*, Princeton.

Thomas, D. (1952) *Collected Poems 1934-1952*, J.M. Dent & Sons.

Thomas, D. (1954) *Under Milk Wood: A Play for Voices*, J.M. Dent & Sons.

Thomas, H. (1996) 'The Cardboard Dog – Looking at Plot' in *Language and Learning* (July/Aug), Questions Publishing.

Thomas, H. (1995) 'Paths to Fantasy' in *Language and Learning* (Sept/Oct), Questions Publishing.

*Thomas, R. (1988) *The Class That Went Wild*, Hutchinson.

*Thomas, R. (1987) *The Runaways*, Hutchinson.

Todorov, T. (1990) *Genres in Discourse*, Cambridge University Press (original publication in French, 1978).

*Tolkien, J.R.R. (1937) *The Hobbit*, Allen & Unwin.

Tomkins, J. (ed.) (1980) *Reader Response Criticism*, John Hopkins.

Toolan, M. (1988) *Narrative: A Critical Linguistic Introduction*, Routledge.

Truffaut, F. (1978) *Hitchcock*, Granada.

*Waddell, M. (1996) *My Aunty Sal and the Mega-sized Moose*, Walker.

*Waddell, M. (1988) *Can't You Sleep, Little Bear?*, Walker.

*Waddell, M. (1986) *The Tough Princess*, Walker.

Wallace, E. (1924) *The Sinister Man*, Hodder and Stoughton.

Warlow, A. (1977) 'Kinds of Fiction: A Hierarchy of Veracity' in Meek, Warlow and Barton.

Waterland, L. (1985) *Read With Me: An Apprenticeship Approach to Reading*, The Thimble Press.

*Wilde, O. (1888) *The Happy Prince and Other Stories*.

Wray, D. and Medwell, J. (1991) *Literacy and Language in the Primary Years*, Routledge.

Note: the symbol * denotes a children's book.

INDEX